SHINRAI

Japanese corporate integrity in a disintegrating Europe

Pernille Rudlin

Pernille Rudlin
Visit my website at www.pernillerudlin.com

First Printing: Feb 2019

ISBN-9781796652239

PREFACE

This book was originally compiled with a Japanese reader in mind, from various articles I wrote that were published over the past ten years in The Nikkei Weekly and Teikoku Databank News.

Reading through them, I thought that there might be a readership for the English language version, particularly for those working for or with Japanese companies.

I hope therefore that you will forgive any parts which explain things that you knew already, and that there are some parts which give you a different perspective on something familiar.

Pernille Rudlin
Norwich, UK, 2019.

CONTENTS

INTRODUCTION TO THE ENGLISH EDITION

The title of this book, *shinrai*, is the Japanese word for "trust". It is composed of two characters, *shin*, meaning "believe", and *rai*, which means "to request". In other words, if you trust someone, you believe they will do what you request. The character for *shin* can be broken down further into components which mean "person" and "word" and the character for *rai* can be broken down into "bundle" and "leaves or pages". It implies communication between people is a fundamental part of building trust, but also getting things done and pulling together.

If I were to capture what I try to do in my work in one phrase, it would be "build trust between Japanese and European cultures." This of course leads to questions of how trust is defined, and therefore how it is built.

Analysing the work I have done with clients, I would say there are five components of building trust in multinational companies. In sequential order they are:

1. Communication
Having a common language is critical – this is why any initiative to help immigrants integrate into a society usually starts with language lessons. The problem for Japan is that for native speakers of European languages, Japanese is one of the most difficult languages to learn and Japanese feel similarly about English. Japanese companies can do more to help

Westerners learn Japanese – an intensive course in Japan is one of the most effective ways to do this. Japanese companies can also communicate better than they do in English – it's not enough to make English the common language or force a minimum English level on employees, management needs to communicate vision, strategy and plans in English more effectively than it currently does.

2. Mutual interests

The Economic Partnership Agreement between Japan and the EU is a classic example of common interests helping to build trust. People have differing degrees of interests, but finding mutual interests means that there is a stable basis for negotiation. Japan wants to sell more cars in Europe, European consumers are happy to have cheaper, good quality Japanese cars. Europe wants to sell more food and drink to Japan, Japanese consumers are happy to have cheaper, good quality European wine and cheese. On a micro level, this is why I always encourage Japanese expatriates in Europe to engage in small talk with their European colleagues – it's a way of discovering mutual interests, which means mutual understanding, compromises and agreements are more easily gained.

3. Processes and regulations

Once you have discovered your mutual interests, you can come to an agreement, but it needs mutually recognised standards to work well. What are the quality and safety standards expected of a car, or a cheese in your respective countries?

When there is a low level of trust, laws, regulations and processes are needed as a fall back. However, both Japanese companies and the European Union are sometimes guilty of becoming bogged down in bureaucracy and process. You have to show you are obeying regulations and following processes in order to be trusted, but ultimately, this is not sufficient. How you do something in terms of your intentions and behaviour towards others is as important as carrying out the process correctly and obeying the law.

4. Reliability & accountability

When you trust someone, it is not only because you believe they will obey the law, but also that they will do what they say they will do. For Japanese companies, this can be hard to define, as the culture is often a family style one, where everyone's roles are vague, with no job descriptions and rely on a seniority-based hierarchy. It's assumed everyone will do whatever necessary, in the best interests of the family. Rules can be bent for family members but this vagueness does not work well in more diverse organisations.

The current fight between Carlos Ghosn and Nissan is focused on processes and regulations. Nissan will try to prove Ghosn flouted Japanese law, but will have to answer questions about its own internal rules. Ghosn will try to prove that he followed both internal and external regulations. But what really seems to be at stake is a loss of mutual trust between Saikawa and other Japanese executives and Ghosn. If you are an insider in a Japanese company, you are trusted as a family member to act in the best interests of the family, and rules can be bent accordingly. But once you are seen as an outsider and acting in your own interests, possibly harming the company, then the rules are applied rigidly - just as the UK is finding out as it negotiates to leave the EU.

5. Vision & Values

This is why you need a clear vision of where the company is going and how you want it to be seen. The vision and values have to be discussed with and shared with employees so they feel they belong. The values will guide them as to how they should behave in order to achieve that vision. If the vision is simply to hit various targets, within the boundaries of rigid rules and processes, without employees engaged with the company values, then the kinds of corporate scandals we have seen in both Japanese and European companies will continue, with catastrophic consequences for trust across societies and cultures.

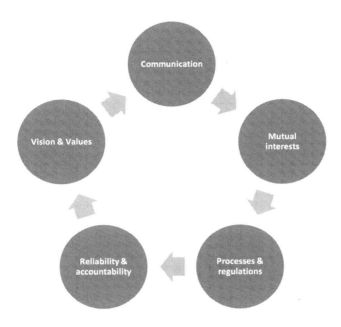

The five elements of building trust across cultures

INTRODUCTION TO THE JAPANESE EDITION

WALLY'S CHILDREN

I was fortunate both when working at Fujitsu in global marketing from 2010–2013 and also afterwards, through my own consultancy, to collaborate with Wally Olins, one of the leading thinkers on corporate identity and branding.

Wally Olins was born in the UK in 1930. He was the son of a Jewish road haulage operator whose ancestors had fled from Russian pogroms to the UK in the 1880s. After graduating from Oxford University, he joined an advertising agency and was posted to India for five years.

As the daughter of an immigrant myself (my mother was born in Denmark) who has also lived outside the UK, I sense that this background gave him an objective, global perspective on British brands. Bored with the traditional advertising-led approach to corporate branding, he founded the ground-breaking brand consultancy Wolff Olins in 1965 and worked with clients such as the Beatles' company Apple, Cunard, British Telecom and the Metropolitan police.

I was one of the last of "Wally's children" as I discovered at the memorial party we were known as. Other Wally's children will recognise his influence in what I have written. Many of the articles that make up this book were published in the Nikkei Weekly and Teikoku Databank magazine during the time I was working with him and Fujitsu global marketing colleagues. His thinking – that branding is not just a logo and that is it is the organising philosophy, which permeates every part of an organisation – the environment, the communication, the behaviour, and the products and services – influenced what we did at Fujitsu. It is also why this book looks at everything from location, corporate social responsibility and governance topics through to HR, management and internal communications.

BREXIT AND BUSINESS TRENDS

Because the articles were written over a period of several years, some of them have been superseded by events. They have therefore been updated and amended, for which I thank my brilliant translator Chigusa Suzuki. We decided to clarify the dates on which they were written, rather than completely re-write them, as the book is also in part an explanation of "what is Europe" for which it is necessary to explain how and why Brexit and other recent developments have evolved.

The first article I wrote about Brexit dates from 2013 (Chapter 5.7), and I am sorry to say that its pessimistic predictions have so far proved correct. In the five years that have passed since, it has become obvious that, even though Brexit has not yet happened, business does not stand still.

Business is like water – it needs to flow, and when it meets obstacles it tries to flow around or over them. It also does not flow uphill. Governments can put dams, dykes and canals in place to guide or stop the flow, but they cannot control events and the British government has been so distracted by the politics of Brexit that it has not been able to build the necessary dams and canals and the ones that it has - like reducing the corporate tax rate to 17% - may even be counterproductive.

The tidal pull for Japanese companies is a strong focus on understanding the customer, and building deep and long-lasting relationships with them, creating strong collaborative eco systems and supply chains. In Japan this is supported by a mutual understanding of the market.

Japanese companies have managed to replicate these supply chains, particularly in the automotive industry, in Europe, but it has come to a point now where the supply chains include many non-Japanese companies, and a deeper understanding of the European market and the European business environment is needed.

EUROPEAN VALUES

It is, however, so hard to come to any general conclusions about the "European" market or workplace. As is seen with Brexit, the Catalan independence movement, the rise of populism in Eastern Europe and Italy, European values (and borders) are hard to pin down and can change.

There are certain elements which I have found common to most European workplaces, and I have tried to explain them here. Some of these elements can be explained by education systems.

Most Europeans have been through an education system which encourages them to engage in "critical thinking". Facts are taught, but rather than the multiple-choice tests of Japanese schools, European children are taught how to write essays, express their opinions and back them up with evidence. European schools also offer drama lessons, public speaking and debating clubs and many teachers prefer the "Socratic" method of teaching whereby they ask questions of their pupils and encourage debate, rather than simply convey facts and processes.

WHAT EUROPEANS THINK OF JAPANESE COLLEAGUES, AND VICE VERSA

I have used this Socratic method in my own seminars. Over the past fifteen years I have asked Japanese working in Europe and Europeans working in Japanese companies what they find most positive and what they find most challenging about their workplaces. The answers show two sides of the same coin.

Europeans appreciate how polite, respectful and calm their Japanese colleagues are. But at the same time, they are frustrated by the lack of a clear yes or no, that disagreements are not expressed, and if they have Japanese juniors on the team, that the juniors do not challenge them, or other Japanese seniors.

Japanese appreciate how Europeans are so accepting of diversity, are able to prioritise what is important to ensure a good work life balance and are rational and logical in debate, but at the same time wonder why Europeans have meetings with endless discussions and no conclusions, will only do what is in their job description and don't seem to have a sense of urgency about meeting deadlines.

These concerns can all be addressed in the workshops I and my team run for Japan Intercultural Consulting (www.japanintercultural.com).

THE NEED FOR A CLEAR STRATEGY AND A STRONG BRAND IN A CHANGING EUROPE

Overall, then, Europeans and Japanese enjoy good workplace relationships. But sometimes, particularly amongst senior Europeans, deeper frustrations come out regarding the direction and strategy of their Japanese company. Generally, Europeans like Japanese companies for having a long-term perspective, strong ethical values and high-quality products and appreciate that their Japanese colleagues are diligent, structured and process oriented in their workstyle. Unfortunately, this sums up almost all Japanese companies, and therefore makes it difficult to discern a distinctive strategy or brand.

A strong brand is needed more than ever in modern Europe. My view is that Brexit is accelerating trends that are already simultaneously disintegrating and integrating the region. The supply chains in the automotive industry are stretching eastwards to Slovakia and the Czech Republic and southwards to north Africa. The balance of power in the supply chains is also shifting away from the car manufacturers and towards the components suppliers and IT companies.

This tendency to both integrate globally, but disintegrate in terms of management and powerbases can also be seen in electronics and IT companies such as Panasonic, Fujitsu, Canon and Sony. The rise of fintech and Brexit-forced moves away from London mean that even the financial services companies which were heavily concentrated in London are shifting part of their operations to Luxembourg, Frankfurt, Brussels, Paris and Amsterdam.

This disintegration needs to be counterbalanced by integration to avoid chaos ensuing. Multinationals have to have a much clearer set of values, understood and acted up on by employees across the world. The brand values need to be clearly communicated to customers too, so that they are reassured that they will get the same standards and quality, wherever they are located.

I will return to what makes a strong brand in the afterword.

CHAPTER 1

GLOBALIZATION OF JAPANESE COMPANIES AND EXPANSION INTO EUROPE

1. LESSONS FROM BREXIT ON MANAGING IN EUROPE

Whatever the outcome of the Brexit negotiations, there are two conclusions we can already draw from what has happened so far in terms of how Japanese businesses may need to respond. One is that structural trends in business which were already apparent in Europe will be accelerated and the second is that differences in negotiating approaches in Europe have not disappeared, despite 25 years of the European Union and single market.

In terms of organisational structure, there is a strange mix of physical disintegration and integration on a virtual level. Currently, over half of the biggest Japanese companies in Europe have their regional headquarters in the UK. This is because of the depth of financial and other support services that are available in the UK, the free movement of people that enables hiring many different nationalities in the UK and the ease of doing business in the English language. The latter advantage will not disappear with Brexit of course, but if the UK does not keep its EU financial 'passport', it's possible a lot of the financial and other services will shift to Amsterdam or Frankfurt. Brexit may also bring an end to the free movement of people between the EU and the UK.

In any case, many of the back office, functional, coordinating jobs were already moving out of the UK. Cheaper, English speaking, well-educated employees can be found elsewhere in the EU. Larger Japanese companies are already developing a pan-European management structure, where teams are scattered across several countries. This is proving very challenging for Japanese employees who are more accustomed to a team working physically together, seated in a cluster of desks. Japanese companies will have to put processes in place to enable discussions and decisions to be made via remote communications and maintain a generous budget for travel.

The second conclusion is that Europe is still split between the pragmatists and the principles and rules-based groups. The pragmatists, often traditional trading nations such as the UK, Netherlands and Denmark, tend to negotiate step by step, concession by concession, whereas Japanese companies prefer to acquire all information and know all the risks before making one big decision. Principles and rules-based countries such as France or Germany clash with the pragmatists because they refuse to make concessions on what they would consider key principles (such as the free movement of people) or deviate from the rules which have been set in place.

This is why the European Union has become bogged down so often in processes and discussions and seems remote, bureaucratic and corrupt to ordinary citizens. There are two further lessons to be learnt from this for business. One is that, no matter what happens in Europe, the British provide an important counterbalance to the French and the Germans in a management team, if you want pragmatic solutions to problems. The second is that management must not become so inward looking that it fails to communicate its vision to the rest of the employees.

2. USING EUROPEAN SUBSIDIARIES AS A GLOBAL PIVOT

Reflecting on the trends of the past 15 years since I founded my business supporting Japanese companies in Europe, the most obvious development has been the increase in major acquisitions by Japanese companies of Europe-based multinationals.

In 2016, Mitsui Sumitomo Insurance Group acquired UK Lloyd's underwriters Amlin for £3.5bn and Hitachi finalised the acquisition in 2015 of AnsaldoBreda and Italian company Finmeccanica's stake in Ansaldo STS, for around €800m.

Both these acquisitions are representative of a structural change I have seen evolving in quite a few Japanese multinationals. Hitachi has moved the global headquarters of its rail business to the UK and it seems the

Japanese insurance majors, who have all now acquired underwriting firms based in the UK, are hoping that their acquisitions will act as pivots for further global expansion.

Clearly Japanese companies are not just buying into a market with their acquisitions, but hoping that they have also acquired global management capability. Whereas in the past there were some examples of Japanese companies using their US subsidiaries to manage the global network, it seems now that Europeans are being asked to manage operations in the US and beyond.

This is partly due to another long-term trend in Japan, which is the lack of "global *jinzai* (human resources)", particularly at senior management level, to manage overseas growth, but it also reflects the fact that European multinationals are used to managing companies scattered across many countries, in a virtual matrix structure. This means the heads of various business units or functions may not all be physically located in the same headquarters. European managers need to have strong, globally effective professional expertise but also good cross-cultural communication skills to be able to manage teams remotely.

Europeans are comfortable with doing this in Europe and to some extent working with the US too. However, working with Japan is still a new experience for most of them. They are often baffled by the fact that their professional expertise and remote communication skills are not enough to persuade or win support from Japan headquarters. Managers in Japan headquarters are only used to communicating with people who are physically present in the office. They tend to be generalists, who do not find arguments grounded solely in expert opinion all that convincing.

Unless conscious effort is made to overcome these communication barriers, Japan headquarters maybe behave like the three monkeys, who see no evil, hear no evil and speak no evil. In Japan my understanding is that this is seen as virtuous behaviour. However, in the West this is seen as ignoring problems and misbehaviour until it is too late.

3. ADDING VALUE

When I approached the US-based founder of Japan Intercultural Consulting fifteen years' ago about setting up a European operation, her immediate reaction was that this was great timing, because she had just had some enquiries from her customers wanting her training in Europe.

This was reassuring to me, as it meant we had an existing customer demand to build on. The other value she was able to add was that Japan Intercultural Consulting has a tried and tested business model and a training format, that I could easily adapt for the European market.

Nonetheless, we have not had quite as many global customers as I was expecting. Ultimately, services businesses like ours are very local and personal – they depend on customer preferences for the actual person delivering the training, and sometimes there are pre-existing personal relationships with other suppliers. Even if Japan headquarters or their US subsidiary suggests to a local HR department in Europe that they use us, there can be resistance and refusal.

We try to make sure that we have trainers who are local to each market and are credible and personable, of course – but again, such people have to be convinced that Japan Intercultural Consulting has something valuable to add before they are willing to give up their autonomy to work for us.

Japanese companies' initial moves into Europe were very customer driven – mostly in a B2B supply chain whether it was automotive or financial or other support services like IT. Those customers have become global in their demands, so Japanese suppliers have had to put together a global, seamless supply chain to meet those demands.

My impression is that more recent entries into Europe are not so customer led, however. The reasons given for acquisition are usually around the company's needs – that the Japanese domestic market is saturated, low growth, the population is ageing and shrinking. All companies like to grow, so the only place to do that is outside Japan.

Many Japanese companies are sitting on big piles of cash, so why not use that money to acquire something with better returns, is the more shareholder driven argument. I worry, however, that if the Japanese company is not adding value to the acquisition, either with an improved business model or bringing new customers to the acquired company, then these assets just pile up, and like old stock in a warehouse, start to lose their marketability.

It might have been better to use that pile of cash to refine the domestic business model first, investing in training and technology to make sure it is as differentiated as possible, and also to research thoroughly customer needs outside Japan, before venturing overseas.

4. TREAT OVERSEAS ACQUISITIONS AS MARRIAGES NOT LODGERS

There was a 33% drop in the number of overseas acquisitions by Japanese companies in the first quarter of 2014 compared to 2013. I viewed this as a temporary blip because of the weakening yen. However, corporate reshuffles at the time showed that senior executives are being asked to step down early if they are perceived to have been responsible for the failure of major overseas acquisitions. So there may be an element of "once bitten, twice shy".

A 2014 survey of 148 leading Japanese companies by The Nikkei indicated there is still an appetite for acquisition. Of the executives polled, 42.6% said they wanted to acquire companies both domestically and abroad, with North America and Europe being the favoured overseas destinations.

One way these executives could do a better job of acquiring overseas companies is to be conscious of the fact that Japanese companies behave like traditional Japanese families – and adapt their acquisition and integration processes accordingly. For example, Japanese families, even to this day, adopt sons-in-law, who take on the family name and become the heir, especially if there is a family business at stake.

Japanese companies seem reluctant to use the "adopted son-in-law" model for their overseas acquisitions. Sometimes the acquisition is more like a marriage – a long courtship of holding an equity stake in a large foreign company and then a final consummation some years later. And like a marriage, this approach requires effort and commitment on both sides, through thick and thin, to build a new family, with a new set of values and customs.

A more prevalent model is treating the acquired overseas company like a lodger in the house, rather than a member of the family. So long as the lodger behaves, with no loud music late at night, and pays the rent on time, they are left to their own devices.

Initially North American and European companies may welcome this approach. They are allowed to continue as before, with plenty of autonomy and not much interference. However, like a lodger, they start to feel isolated from the family activities, and wonder whether they should be looking to move out to better lodgings. Or they may hit financial difficulties and stop paying the rent, at which point the Japanese landlord cracks down hard.

When North American and European companies acquire other companies, some attention is at least nominally paid to the cultural aspects, but the main focus is on integration or imposition of systems, structures, policies and targets. The acquired company is usually left in no doubt as to how they are going to have to adapt to the new parent, well before the ink is dry on the purchase agreement.

If Japanese companies do not feel comfortable with this clinical approach, then a lot more thought needs to go into how exactly their new overseas subsidiary can be a true adopted son and heir – or spouse.

5. M&A AND TAX INCENTIVES

The front pages of the British business press in early 2014 were full of debate about whether to welcome or be worried by the US pharmaceutical company Pfizer's bid to take over AstraZeneca, a UK-Swedish company. The £63bn bid would have made it the biggest foreign takeover of a British company in history.

Initially the British government wanted to portray the bid as a vote of confidence in what they had done to make Britain an attractive destination for foreign investment. However, the former CEO of AstraZeneca, Sir David Barnes, said that he was concerned that Pfizer would "act like a praying mantis and suck the lifeblood out of their prey." Pfizer wanted to move its tax domicile to Britain when it acquired AstraZeneca, to take advantage of the UK's low corporate tax rate and what is called a "patent box", which gives tax breaks for research.

If Pfizer want these tax incentives, it should invest in the UK itself, and not attempt to do it via a takeover, Sir David argued. Pfizer last hit the headlines in the UK when it closed down its 60-year-old research facilities in the east of England, with the loss of nearly 2000 jobs, in 2011. A few years before that it closed R&D sites in Nagoya, Japan and the US. The reasoning at the time was that research was better outsourced to smaller companies.

I have not heard anyone say that this trend has reversed, yet AstraZeneca had committed to investing £500 million in a new research facility and headquarters in Cambridge, which is the main science cluster in the UK. Pfizer said it would honour this investment, and the jobs that depend on it, for five years at least.

The consensus in the UK seemed to be that given Pfizer's "accounting led" approach, such commitments may not be worth much. The US company Kraft also promised it would not cut jobs when it took over one of the UK's most famous companies, the chocolate manufacturer Cadburys, in 2010, and then shortly after closed down one of its factories.

This does not mean that the UK is hostile to all foreign takeovers, however. Japanese companies are much more welcome, as they are seen as having long term commitment to their investments. Takeda's acquisition of Swiss company Nycomed did lead to job losses but this was seen as inevitable after a merger. It is the wholesale closure of a factory or R&D site with major impact on the community around it which troubles people in Europe.

Many of the British researchers laid off by Pfizer in 2011 have found jobs in small start-ups, but not everyone can be an entrepreneur or has the personal resilience to go through the trauma of redundancy. When I ask participants in my training what they like about working in a Japanese company, they almost always mention the stability, the long-term view and the loyalty of the company to its staff. Large, stable employers are important for the health of the community, whatever the country of origin.

6. GLOBAL STANDARDIZATION CAN MEAN SWALLOWING YOUR PRIDE

The European senior management team of a business which had been newly acquired by a Japanese company complained to me about being treated as if Europe was one homogenous country, when in fact they only had offices in 5 very different countries in Europe, with a headquarters in Germany. "It's true, we know how to work with each other in Europe – after all Europeans have been living and working together for hundreds of years, but it seems strange that on paper we're supposed to be a tri-regional structure of Europe, North America and Asia, and yet North America has only two employees and Asia has no regional headquarters, with Taiwan, China, Korea and Japan being managed separately"

This was just a small company, but actually I have seen similar situations in many other much larger Japanese multinationals. It's partly that Europeans are very sensitive to their status – and want to be treated on a par with other regional heads – and to them this means the European definition of regions, with Asia as one region.

But it's also due to a justifiable concern that if the company is meant to be offering global products and services, it needs to have a well-balanced global structure operating off common platforms, systems and processes. If the company grows by acquisition, you often end up with very different portfolios of services and products from country to country, incompatible processes and systems and no clear idea of how revenue and costs should be shared across the regions which are contributing to the global offering.

This can cause huge, long running arguments, partly because standardizing trade, production processes and technology are interrelated issues. Once you decide what products and services are global and what are local, you have the basis for splitting revenue accordingly. But you have to be careful this does not lead to regional organisations focusing on their local products and services, refusing to participate in global contracts because they make more profit out of local contracts.

Once you know what you are offering globally, you can standardise the technology – such as having all the company's websites running off the same content management system, or production running off the same platforms or sales and purchasing using the same global accounting system.

Sometimes Japan headquarters has to swallow their pride for the sake of speed and efficiency. I was impressed that Nomura, when it acquired Lehman Brothers, decided to move their dealing onto the Lehman platform, because they judged it to be technically superior and faster than trying to integrate platforms or shift everyone onto the Japanese system.

Nobody wants to deal with these problems because they are so complex and lead to fights and easy resistance by those claiming that the global standard is not going to work in their markets. But unfortunately, if you do not deal with these issues soon after an acquisition, they fester and become even more difficult to resolve.

7. WHERE TO BASE YOUR EUROPEAN HEADQUARTERS

According to my company's Top 30 Japanese employers in Europe, Middle East & Africa rankings, over half have their regional headquarters based in the UK. The other popular bases are Germany, Netherlands and Belgium.

Of course, there are many Japanese companies who do not have a European headquarters, but the trend among those who have been in Europe for a longer period is unmistakably towards consolidating across Europe in terms of functional areas such as purchasing or HR or finance. This seems to be to the benefit of the UK, which is the undoubted European if not world capital of professional services - with many globally capable financial, marketing, legal, consulting and HR firms in London.

The UK has long been a favourite destination for Japanese foreign direct investment, for various reasons ranging from the English language, to golf to the UK's open economy. Germany has also been very popular, particularly with Japanese engineering companies who feel an affinity with German process orientation and risk aversion, as well as having historical ties such as Fujitsu with Siemens or Denso with Bosch. The North Rhine Westphalia region was particularly active since the 1960s in encouraging Japanese companies to set up there, although Sony decided initially to set up in Berlin, largely, it was rumoured, because of Norio Ohga's love of the Berlin Philharmonic.

The Netherlands became popular because of the tax advantages offered, and also, along with Belgium, was an obvious logistical centre for Europe. Lately, however, there seems to be a shift of these headquarters to the UK. Canon has moved from the Netherlands to Uxbridge, near London. Denso and Bosch announced their break up in 2012, and although Denso continues to be headquartered in the Netherlands, there seem to be several senior managers with European roles based in the UK. Fujitsu and Siemens parted ways in 2009, with the Fujitsu European operations being split between Continental Europe, the Nordics, and UK and Ireland, then consolidated into Europe, Middle East, India and Africa, run by the former MD of the UK operation.

Sony sold its Berlin headquarter building in 2008 and then consolidated its sales and marketing across Europe, based in Weybridge, a few kilometres south west of London. However, it seems to be shifting towards a "virtual" European structure, with shared HR services now set up in Turkey, and individual senior executives with European remits being based in whatever location they prefer. This pattern has also become evident in other IT and telecoms companies such as NTT Data.

Even this virtual European company structure seems to benefit the UK the most, as senior executives of all nationalities are can be found in, or seem relatively happy to relocate to, London and its suburbs. With more than 40% of London's population were born outside the UK, London has truly become a global capital and a place to develop global careers.

8. GERMANY AND THE SHIFT OF MANUFACTURING TO THE EAST

Germany has historically been the main rival to the UK in Europe for Japanese investment. The UK absorbs about 40% of total Japanese investment into the EU but according to the Japanese Ministry of Foreign Affairs, there are actually 50% more Japan originated companies (703) in Germany compared to the UK (471)[1].

The reason for this discrepancy in numbers may be to do with the difference in the sectors that are investing in Germany and the UK and also the scale of the companies that are being acquired. According to my own research there are more employees on average at Japan affiliated companies in the UK than there are for Japan affiliated companies in Germany.

This may be because the big employers - Japanese car manufacturers - do not have production in Germany - unlike the UK with Nissan, Honda and Toyota. There are plenty of Japanese automotive component manufacturers, but they tend to be what is known in German as "Mittelstand" or medium sized companies.

Manufacturing represents around 20% of German GDP, similar to Japan. Germany has of course always had a strong reputation for engineering and German cultural values such as risk aversion and process orientation fit well with Japanese corporate mindsets.

By contrast, only 11% of the UK's GDP is derived from manufacturing and 80% of UK GDP is services, particularly financial services such as banking and insurance. This sector accounts for quite a few of the Japanese companies who have multiple subsidiaries in the UK, as well as trading companies, holding companies and services companies providing financing and other functions across Europe.

---

[1] Japanese and British government officials and ministers usually say there are around 1000 Japanese companies in the UK. According to the Japanese Ministry of Foreign Affairs in 2018, there are 986 Japanese companies in the UK, but this includes the multiple branches, representative offices and joint ventures of the same companies and also companies which were established by Japanese permanent residents in the UK.

This might explain why the UK has more Japanese residents than Germany – around 63,000 compared to 46,000 in Germany - many are perhaps acting as liaison and coordinators with Japan HQ for the region. However, this number is falling for the UK, and increasing for Germany.

Does this mean that the UK is losing its role as the services centre for the region to Germany? Looking at the detail, it seems the main factor behind the drop in the number of Japanese in the UK is that there are 3,000 fewer Japanese students and academics in the UK compared to a year ago.

Intra company transferee numbers are rising for both countries, but by 4.2% on last year for Germany, compared to 2.6% for the UK.

Looking at the recent investments into the UK and Germany, the trends of the past few years still seem to hold. Investments into the UK are in the form of establishing regional holding companies, or M&A in biotech, information technology and services for the UK market such as car parking. Investments into Germany are mainly for the wholesale of electronic components and machinery. Sometimes these are German sales offices for Japanese companies who already have sales or manufacturing in the UK. As manufacturing shifts eastward in Europe, so the sales hubs are moving with them.

9. LOCATING YOUR OFFICE IN THE UK, VIRTUAL OR OTHERWISE

A few years ago, I took advantage of the quiet period of August, when most Europeans go on holiday for two to four weeks, to move my home office into a building at the bottom of our garden. It was to prepare for employing someone for the first time. The room in our house I was using as an office was too small for two people.

This kind of set up may be unusual in Japan, but it is increasingly common in the UK. Over half of British SMEs (2.5 million) are run from the owner's home. It is cheaper of course not to have to rent an office, with all the attendant overheads. It's also much easier and cheaper from a human resource management perspective if all staff are freelance, working from their homes, rather than employees. However, I really felt I had reached the limit of how far I could grow the business without having a deputy, who is physically in the same room as me.

Most Japanese companies starting up in the UK will want a physical, rather than virtual, presence of course. In terms of location, for manufacturing, proximity to customer plants, or logistical hubs will be a key consideration. For the services sector in the UK, being able to access London easily is very important, as so many clients are based there, and there are many useful networking events and support organisations in the capital.

Central London is very expensive, so unless a prestigious address is expected by clients and employees (the financial sector would be a typical example of when this would be the norm) it is probably better to be located in the suburbs or the various towns surrounding London in the South East.

I was fortunate in that I already lived in the South East, in a town which contains the global headquarters of several multinationals such as Unilever and Exxon. There are serviced offices in my town and also neighbouring towns, with prices starting from around £200 per person per month, which includes most overheads such as utilities, furniture, receptionists etc.

Many of these are shared, open plan spaces however, in business parks. I felt ultimately this would not be the right atmosphere for me to work productively, and might also not be very appealing to whomever I hire.

This is the other factor in choosing an office - whether employees will be attracted, or deterred, by what your offices look like and where they are located. Business parks are often a long way from any shops or restaurants, and require a car to commute to. Many employees in the South East of the UK commute for over an hour to get to these business parks, by train or car, but the most attractive employers usually provide excellent facilities such as restaurants or a gym, to compensate for the isolated environment.

I wasn't offering a gym or restaurant in my office at the end of the garden of course, but I made sure to have a good coffee making machine!

10. 4 CULTURES OF CONTROLLING OVERSEAS SUBSIDIARIES

In a trip to Japan in 2017 I visited Amazon's offices to have lunch with an acquaintance who has been working there for 1 year and 3 months. He told me that Amazon has expanded so rapidly this past year that he is now in the upper half of a chart which shows all employees ranked by their length of time working for the company.

He also told me that almost all the non-Japanese people working there were, like him, locally hired and that there were hardly any expatriate staff from the US headquarters. I therefore wondered how Amazon HQ could control a subsidiary which is growing so rapidly without any expatriate managers to keep monitor it.

Amazon also tries to minimize the number of processes and procedures it has, in order to maintain the speedy, fast to market, start-up mentality it had when it first began over twenty years' ago.

In the various multinationals and their subsidiaries I have worked in or with, you can usually find three types of headquarter control. American, sales focused companies tend to control their subsidiaries by setting numerical targets. If the subsidiary employees and managers hit the targets, they get bonuses, if they miss them, they get fired. Many multinationals who are not American in origin use these systems because numbers are easy for everyone to understand, regardless of language.

Another way of managing subsidiaries which both European and American multinationals also use is to ensure compliance through having strong regulations, processes and systems, and clear hierarchical chains of command, so everyone knows who has responsibility and authority for each part of the business.

A third way, which is more common among Japanese companies and also companies such as the German Mittelstand and family owned companies, is "control by the family" – in other words members of the headquarters family are sent out to subsidiaries to monitor what is going on and promote the corporate culture.

My Amazon contact explained that Amazon ensures its employees behave in compliance with Amazon's core values by having a very rigorous hiring process. Candidates are interviewed several times by multiple employees and asked questions about past experiences, to reveal what kind of mindset they have.

I can imagine, however, that it is difficult for Japanese companies to use this method if their overseas subsidiaries were the result of an acquisition, or if the company has already been operating overseas for several decades. There will already be a substantial legacy of staff who may have rather different values and behaviours to those of the Japanese headquarters.

It would also be a mistake, and damaging to the benefits of having diverse, localised operations that are close to their customers, to impose too rigid a set of behaviours and values on all overseas employees.

Nonetheless, I strongly recommend that Japanese companies who are about to acquire or set up operations overseas ensure they have a clear, globally understandable company mission and values and hire or promote their overseas employees accordingly.

CHAPTER 2
HIRING AND RETAINING
EMPLOYEES IN EUROPE

1. COMMON TRAPS FOR RECRUITING IN EUROPE FOR JAPAN RELATED COMPANIES

A couple of years ago my business had expanded sufficiently that I needed to hire someone to support me. Three months later, I failed to recruit anyone.

In reflecting on why I was not able to hire someone, and what I needed to do next, I realised that I was in danger of falling into the same traps that I have often seen Japanese companies in Europe slide into.

The first trap is being attracted to Japanese speakers without considering their skills and your business's needs more carefully. It's easy to find Japanese speakers in the UK – there are over 60,000 Japanese people living in the UK now – many are students or expatriates but there are also residents who have settled here, often married to British people.

In addition to this, there are around 6,000 members of the Japan Exchange and Teaching programme UK alumni association. These are British or other English-speaking nationals who have worked in Japan for 1 to 3 years or more, usually in a school or in local government. Most of them fall in love with Japan as a result, and want to pursue careers where they can continue to have contact with Japan and use their Japanese language ability.

The second trap is to hire Japanese people (usually women) and JET alumni into general office administration roles, somewhat vaguely defined, to cover everything from receptionist to HR to translation work. This often leads to frustration on both sides. Japanese women begin to suspect that they are being treated like second class Office Ladies, and when they complain to their British husbands about the overtime or the menial tasks they are asked to do, their husbands often urge them to raise a grievance dispute with their employer.

JET alumni begin to worry that there is no career progression or professional development. Many of them come to me, asking what they should do, and I always advise – find a profession you feel suited to first, like law or accountancy, and then find a way to connect back to Japan.

In both cases, some of the disappointment can be avoided by having a clear job description and a proper contract, and for the Japanese company to be realistic and open about what kind of expectations both parties should have as to how the job can develop. If possible, they should provide or support training where needed, and remember to revise the job description accordingly, as the employee progresses.

So, if I was to take my own medicine, I should have been more clear and focused on the support skills I needed, which were primarily invoicing, chasing payments, paying suppliers and some management accounting (forecasting cash flows etc). This does not require a Japanese speaker, fun though it would have been to have a likeminded person to work with.

2. THE SKILLS SHORTAGE IN EUROPE

Seven in ten British employers have been having difficulties in filling vacancies, and 40% say it has become harder over the past year to find the staff they need, according to a recent survey of 1000 companies by the Chartered Institute of Personnel Development and Adecco, a staffing company.

The situation has been exacerbated by Brexit. The numbers of workers born abroad in Britain fell by 58,000 year on year, whereas it had increased 263,000 over the previous 12-month period. This was mainly due to a drop in the number of workers coming to the UK from the EU.

It's not just a UK problem, however. According to a JETRO survey at the end of 2017, "securing human resources" was the number one operational challenge for Japanese companies in Europe. This includes Germany, the Netherlands and even Central and Eastern European countries such as Hungary and the Czech Republic.

So how can Japanese companies compete with local employers chasing the same skilled workforce?

I like to use a model developed by Fons Trompenaars and Charles Hampden-Turner to explain to Japanese companies where they can win as an employee brand.[2] It's a matrix, based on degree of hierarchy and degree of task versus relationship orientation, resulting in four corporate cultures – the Guided Missile, The Eiffel Tower, the Incubator and the Family.

Guided Missiles are typical American, sales-oriented organisations where the employees are motivated by targets, achievement and reward.

The **Eiffel Tower** organisation is more hierarchical, focused on structure. People are motivated by their status in the organisational hierarchy and promises of promotion.

Many people in Europe are used to the Eiffel Tower style of company and when they join a Japanese company, they are concerned by the lack of defined paths to progress their career and also an absence of clear, strategic direction.

Other Europeans, particularly in the R&D, creative, IT, design and engineering sectors, are more used to the **Incubator** type of company. Here the main motivation is not money or status, but rather developing and using one's skills to innovate.

Most Japanese companies belong to the **Family** style company. Employees want to contribute to the longevity and good reputation of the family, as a respected family member. It is difficult for Family style companies to motivate employees with money or status, as these are dependent on seniority, rather than performance.

Japanese companies in Europe have a reputation for good benefits, but only average pay. There is also a sense that there is a limit to how far you can be promoted if you are not Japanese - in other words, a family member.

Japanese companies are appealing to Europeans because they are "different" and "interesting" and also because they are seen as good corporate citizens. But Europeans also need to be made to feel it is possible to become a family member, by helping them understand the company's vision and values – including through secondments to Japan headquarters – if you want to retain them.

---

[2]Riding the Waves of Culture: Understanding Cultural Diversity in Business, *Fons Trompenaars & Charles Hampden Turner*, (Nicholas Brearley: 2003), 159

3. THE RECRUITMENT INDUSTRY IN EUROPE

The two newest entrants in the rankings that my company compiles of the biggest Japanese employers in the UK are both recruitment agencies – Trust Tech and Outsourcing. Both companies have acquired several recruitment agencies in the UK - as well as in Germany, Netherlands and Poland - over the past 4 years.

This is bringing back memories for me of 13 years' ago when I acted as consultant to another Japanese recruitment agency, who had acquired several companies in the UK and Eastern Europe. They asked me to find ways in which these companies could cooperate and collaborate with each other, to enable a more integrated structure and strategy in Europe.

I quickly found, however, that each recruitment market in Europe was very local, with their own customs, laws and regulations. The Japanese company ultimately withdrew from Europe, as it had itself been acquired by a bigger Japanese recruitment company and its strategic focus became much more domestic oriented.

It is not clear what the strategic intention of the Japanese recruitment companies in expanding in Europe is this time, beyond growth in turnover. They mention providing manufacturing and IT staff to Japanese customers who have operations overseas, but I'm guessing this is more likely to be in Asia than Europe.

Japanese manufacturing in Europe is moving eastwards, so having a presence in Poland, Czech Republic or Slovakia may well be useful in assisting Japanese companies there.

As for the UK, there is a shortage of people with engineering and IT skills and this looks set to worsen, thanks to Brexit potentially restricting rights of EU citizens to live and work in the UK. The number of people coming to the UK from the EU has already fallen dramatically, causing labour shortages in healthcare, construction and food processing sectors.

Apart from the impact of Brexit, the main change in the UK recruitment sector in the past decade is the increase in regulation and compliance. The reason that Japanese recruitment companies suddenly find themselves amongst the biggest Japanese employers in the UK is that temporary workers are now considered under law as employees of the staffing agency, and have rights accordingly to pensions and other benefits. Staffing agencies must therefore comply with UK legislation such as reporting on the gender pay gap and complying with the EU's General Data Protection Regulation.

Industry experts say that recruitment in Europe is no longer about just sourcing candidates and placing them. Labour shortages and pressures to hire people with more diverse backgrounds mean that recruiters have to be more innovative and better at gaining insights from data, to help their customers revise job roles, benefits and salaries to make themselves more attractive.

This means being as close as possible to the customer and the local pool of potential recruits. I am not sure therefore, how Japanese companies can add value to this sector in Europe, or indeed learn from it. So maybe their acquisitions are just about growing revenue, after all.

4. IS IT WORTH THE EFFORT TO LEARN JAPANESE?

When people hear that I speak Japanese they usually say "how amazing – you must be so clever" and "you must be in demand for all sorts of jobs". Actually, I learnt Japanese the stupid way, which was to live in Japan as a child, and go to a Japanese school. And as for being in demand, I find that most companies do not want a Japanese specialist as a full-time employee.

So, I recommend to Japanese speakers that they think about what profession or industry they want to be in first, and then look for ways to incorporate their language skills. Most companies rightly put a priority on people's technical or interpersonal skills rather than a specific language ability.

It's true that Japanese companies and people who supply services to them outside of Japan often hire Japanese speakers – but this can end in frustration if the Japanese speaker is simply given a nebulous role as a translator/customer liaison/interpreter with no clear career path.

Non-Japanese people working in Japanese companies often ask me if it's worth learning Japanese themselves. I always say yes, although I warn them that they may get very frustrated if they expect a lesson a week to lead to fluency. Once they discover the three different ways of writing and multiple levels of politeness, not to mention the countless ways of counting, it's very easy to give up in despair.

Even if it doesn't have an immediate result, I encourage Japanese companies to fund employees' efforts to learn Japanese, because there is more and more evidence to show that learning another language helps you understand the culture and even unconsciously adapt the way you behave – how you analyse and react to situations.

For example, the Japanese language is "selfless", which is a core Japanese value too. A typical English sentence has a "Subject, Verb, Object" construction. "I love you" for example. But in Japanese there is often no subject, and even no object. You just say "love", and the context provides all the clues. This is another Japanese communication trait – to be "high context" – to understand what is not being said, and be sensitive to the context.

Having multilingual employees is a benefit not just because they may understand Japanese corporate cultures better. Recent research in neuroscience shows that multilingual people's brains operate differently. For example, they make more rational decisions if they are functioning in a non-primary language. Working in another language reduces loss aversion, so people become better at assessing risks and benefits.

My observation, having worked with hundreds of Japanese companies in Europe over the past 12 years is that they tend to hire proportionately more multilingual employees than domestic European companies do. Perhaps they instinctively realise that multilingual people, even if Japanese is not one of their languages, are more likely to have the abilities to manage complexity and problem solve that they are looking for.

5. THE MILLENNIAL GENERATION AND JOB MOBILITY

European employers, just as in Japan, are worrying about how to manage and motivate the so-called millennial generation – people who were born between the early 1980s and the 1990s.

Across the world, one characteristic that unites the millennial generation is, of course, a high use of social media. There is some evidence that this has led to a more open-minded attitude to the rest of the world. In the UK, the millennial generation is much more pro-European Union and pro-migrant than the older generations. Millennials are used to building relationships with people they have never met, through mutual interests and hobbies, regardless of their location or nationality or gender.

This has translated into a higher desire than other generations to live, work or study outside their home country. 71% of millennials, regardless of gender, want to work outside their home country during their career, according to a global survey by PwC in 2015. A multigenerational global survey by PwC in the same year showed that all age groups and genders overwhelmingly agreed that secondment early in a career was also critical.

Yet I have seen surveys of Japanese millennials which show that fewer of them are studying abroad or want to be seconded overseas than previous generations. I expect their concern, which is also the top concern of other nationalities, is what their role will be when they are repatriated to their home country.

I suspect there are also assumptions being made on the employer side about who an expatriate should be and what the role should involve. A British academic who had interviewed various Japanese women living in the UK told me she found that many of them joined a Japanese company in Japan, in the expectation that they would be posted overseas. Yet their requests to be seconded were ignored, so they quit their companies and moved abroad themselves.

It seems to me that many of the issues Japanese companies are facing such as attracting and retaining younger people, an ageing workforce or a lack of men or women who can take up global management roles could be resolved by having a more integrated and inclusive approach to job mobility. It is quite normal for European companies to hire graduates from across Europe, and then rotate them around their operations in different countries. A few of our larger clients are now rotating their graduates to Japan too. Global roles do not have to be for 3-5 years in another country – they can be permanent, a few months or indeed a virtual global role.

6. WHY JAPANESE COMPANIES DON'T USE LINKEDIN (BUT SHOULD)

Panasonic, Mitsubishi Estate and Rakuten announced in 2014 that they were going to make use of social networking site LinkedIn for recruitment outside Japan, including Europe. LinkedIn is the world's largest professional networking site, based in California, with more than 460 million users worldwide, so it certainly represents an effective way to identify and attract new recruits.

I have been a member for nearly 15 years, not to find a job, but to network with my European contacts in Japanese companies. It has been noticeable, however, that Japanese employees and Japanese companies in general are not very active on LinkedIn, even though LinkedIn launched a Japanese version and set up an office in Tokyo in 2011.

I assume this is primarily because LinkedIn is used for mid-career hiring and job seeking, which is still not a popular activity in Japan. Indeed, many Europeans dislike to display their skills and experience publicly, and signal thereby that they may be "for hire". Based on my own analysis, the British and Dutch are not so cautious, whereas the privacy conscious (and possibly less comfortable in English) Germans and French hold back.

Many of my German contacts use Xing, a Germany based social networking site instead and the French use Viadeo. However, all Europeans (and people in multinationals in emerging markets such as Turkey) are aware of LinkedIn, and will take a look at it when they are considering moving to another company.

In other words, from an employer perspective, LinkedIn is a tool not just for searching for recruits based on skills and experience, but also for the company to present an attractive profile.

I recommend that any Japanese company reviewing their LinkedIn presence first of all ensure that the "official" company LinkedIn page is clearly labelled as official (to distinguish it from an alumnus site page run by an individual), and employees are encouraged to link their personal LinkedIn profiles to this official page.

More often than not, there are several pages already existing for the Japanese company. This needs to be tidied up, so that there is a headquarters page (in English), and any regional company pages are clearly identified as such. It is possible to interlink the regional company pages to the headquarters page, to show they all belong to the same company family.

These official pages need to be managed by someone either in marketing or HR at the headquarters and regional subsidiaries. They need a description of the company, including size, activities and a link to the correct website. The pages also need to be "branded" to look visually appealing and reflect the company image. Use should be made of the facility to add descriptions of products and services and add news about the company.

If this is done correctly, then "followers" of company will swiftly increase, both from potential recruits and also current employees, who will feel much happier now their employer has a clear and attractive LinkedIn presence they can associate themselves with.

7. HIRING EXPERIENCED AND SKILLED EMPLOYEES - OR TRAIN YOUR OWN

I was surprised when the Japanese expatriate manager at a Japanese logistics firm told me that he thought British logistics was more advanced than logistics in Japan. When I returned to the UK after working in Japan for four years at the end of the 1990s, I remember thinking that there was a real business opportunity for a delivery service in the UK similar to Japan's *takkyubin*. This thought came to me as I watched an enormous container lorry reverse very cautiously up the 19th century narrow alleyway to my London apartment, when all they were delivering was a small armchair. Surely in Japan this would have been delivered in a much smaller van, and within a much shorter time frame, so I would not have had to wait in all day for delivery.

Thanks to the rise of internet shopping (the British are the biggest web shoppers in Europe, apparently) and also the liberalisation of postal services, *takkyubin* type services like MyHermes have now appeared in the UK. You can book a time slot for next day pick up from your house, online, and the prices are cheaper than taking it to the post office, for heavier items.

I assume that similar services are available from *takkyubin* companies in Japan, so I suppose what the Japanese logistics manager was referring to was the higher volume end of logistics in the UK – transporting large quantities of car parts across Europe, for example.

Although it is possible to get qualifications and even university degrees in logistics in the UK, all the British employees of the Japanese firm at which the Japanese manager worked were in agreement that expertise in logistics was only really developed through practical experience, over time, rather than learning the latest theories in the classroom. In that sense, they were much more in alignment with Japanese apprenticeship style "on the job" training approaches.

As the Japanese manager himself pointed out, the firm's employees were very indigenous British. Normally when I do training sessions for Japanese companies in the UK who are in the financial or commercial sectors, more than half the employees are not British.

Maybe for those types of companies, attitude and ability to learn are more important than local market expertise, skills and experience. But for logistics and other traditional, highly skilled industries such as engineering, it is tempting to choose someone who already has the local understanding and the expertise and skills born of experience, rather than train someone up.

Such people are scarce in the UK and the rest of Europe however, and instead we have a stubborn youth unemployment problem, of young people who would rather do physical work, or work outside an office, but have not had the training or experience and cannot find stable jobs.

No wonder then that Hitachi Rail has teamed up with other companies to set up a new University Technical College in the north of England. Apparently they were worried they might have to poach employees from nearby Nissan, otherwise.

8. EUROPEANS VALUE LONG TERM JOB SECURITY AND STABILITY OF JAPANESE COMPANIES

An HR director at a British multinational recently acquired by a Japanese company told me she was baffled by the response from Japan to her department's enquiry regarding the company car grade allocation for a group of Japanese expatriate managers being transferred to work in the UK. All they sent back was a list of the managers' names and their ages, she said.

Of course, this is perfectly understandable once you know about the seniority-based pay and benefits system in Japanese companies. In European companies, salaries and benefits are based on the job role – how high up the managerial ladder you are and the content of the job – with very little attention paid to age or length of service.

Most of the Japanese subsidiaries I work with in Europe have salary and welfare schemes that are locally appropriate. However, there are several aspects of the Japanese HR system which impact employees in Europe, beyond company car grades for expat managers

One aspect is the culture of lifetime employment and the sense of a duty of care for employees. Many Europeans have noticed that Japanese companies are very reluctant to fire even the most poorly performing employee, whether they are European or Japanese. While Europeans are sympathetic to this compassionate stance, they point out it does make performance management for the rest of the team difficult. If poor performers are still on the team, it is demotivating for the other team members.

The other aspect, which is said to be behind Hitachi's announcement in 2014 that it will end seniority based pay for managers, is that the uniqueness of the Japanese HR system hinders job mobility across borders. Most non-Japanese multinationals try to have an internal vacancy system, where employees in all countries are able to apply for job openings across the world. This necessitates detailed job descriptions, and a certain level of unified grading, so employees can assess which jobs are likely to be open to them.

Europeans find it very confusing that Japanese expatriates are assigned to their offices without any seeming regard for whether they have the right qualifications, skills or experience for the role.

My hope for Japanese companies is that they will send more of their overseas employees to Japan HQ. I suspect the Hitachi announcement, coming as it does after two years of having built up an international database of their employees, is that they too are hoping a more unified system will allow employees to transfer all around the world and not just from Japan, and that this will be based on competency rather than just personal development needs and whose turn it is.

But I have to say I also hope that Japanese companies, if they follow Hitachi's suit, do not lose their compassion and loyalty towards their employees as they globalize. Despite all the frustrations it brings, Europeans still prefer the long-term security of working for a Japanese company.

9. EUROPEAN HOLIDAY ALLOWANCES

The announcement in 2015 by the Japanese government that they want to revise the Labour Standards Law to require companies to ensure that workers take their paid leave allowance has attracted a fair amount of attention in European media. Japanese employees are entitled to an average of around 18.5 days a year but typically only take around 9 days.

Japanese employees are admired for the dedication to work shown by the long hours they put in, but many European managers, particularly Germans, worry that overtime is also a sign of poor management, or could lead to health and safety problems if workers do not take time off to "refresh" themselves.

Europeans are much keener than Japanese or Americans to take their full allocation of vacation days. EU legislation mandates that all 28 member countries must by law grant all employees least 4 weeks' holiday. The implementation of this legislation varies greatly from country to country however.

The French and the Nordic countries are famous in Europe for taking the most holidays. One survey showed that the French take all 30 of the days they are statutorily entitled to (this includes Saturdays). They can add up to a further 22 days of holiday as compensation if they work more than 35 hours a week.

Nordic countries have 25–30 days entitlement, and there is an almost universal summer holiday from early June through to the middle of August when most families disappear to the coast or to an island for the whole of the summer.

In Germany, there is a variation from state to state beyond the statutory minimum of 24 days for workers, because each federal state sets additional public holidays and determines the school vacation periods.

We British like to think of ourselves as the most hardworking of the European nations. Although 28 calendar days are statutorily guaranteed, this can include public holidays. The norm for most companies is to offer 25 days, in addition to the 8 or 9 public holidays. There is a trend now for British companies to offer a menu of employee benefits, which includes the ability to buy and sell days of holiday allowances. Unused holidays can also be carried over to the next year, but there is usually a cap on the number of days.

British school summer holidays are much shorter than in Nordic countries and residential children's camps are not as commonly used in

Europe as in the US, so parents do expect to be able to take at least two weeks' break in the summer time to holiday with their children.

Consequently, if you are running a pan-European company or team, you have to put mechanisms in place for employees in many different countries to book their holidays well in advance, so that there is sufficient staff cover even during peak holiday times. Furthermore, there are concerns now that even when on holiday, conscientious employees are checking their smartphones for work email. Daimler hit the news headlines in 2014 for implementing a system which auto deletes emails during vacation times, to make sure employees relax properly.

10. WHY THE BRITISH AND THE JAPANESE ARE LESS PRODUCTIVE THAN THE DUTCH

When I visited the Netherlands a couple of years ago, one of the Japanese managers I met said his main concern was how to motivate his staff. I hear this question often from Japanese managers working in Europe, and I always want to ask – what do you mean by motivation – what would it look like?

Usually a motivated employee is thought to be an employee who makes an effort and perseveres. This is hard to measure objectively, and it is a worry amongst Europeans that Japanese managers evaluate employee motivation by how many hours employees are at their desk. This is a justified concern, reinforced by a report I heard regarding a Japanese GM in Spain who was worrying why his Spanish staff were away from their desks far more than Japanese or even British staff.

If you ask Dutch people what motivates them, according to a long-standing Japanese resident in the Netherlands, they will say "boss, just don't waste my time." In other words, the main way to demotivate the Dutch is to waste their time.

The Dutch have high productivity (usually defined as GDP per hour worked), and also the happiest children, according to various OECD and UNICEF surveys. The connection between the two is pretty obvious when you look out of the window in Amsterdam – the streets are full of mothers and fathers on their bikes, with their children in little carts or on a tandem, going to and from school. Dutch families like to eat supper, together, at 6pm. They also like to spend the evenings doing sports or other hobbies – and allow their children plenty of freedom to come and go as they please. The streets and housing seem clean, safe and spacious, with offices, schools and housing all mixed together, so commuting time is relatively short.

The Dutch people I met said it was quite normal to work one or two days at home, particularly those who had jobs which required regional or global coordinating activities, so didn't need to be in the office to see their team. It is also quite normal for men and women to work part time if they have children, but retain their management roles. So in other words the best way to motivate Dutch employees is to ensure they feel productive – that they can get a lot done in a short amount of time.

However, I overheard a pair of British managers in the hotel at breakfast talking about their Dutch colleagues. They agreed – "the trouble is, although the Dutch are efficient at getting things done, they just wander off on their own and do it, and you end up with everyone going their own way, it's really hard to coordinate."

Maybe this is why Japanese and British productivity, particularly in the services sector, is lower than the Dutch. We spend a lot of time coordinating and monitoring other people's work rather than producing added value ourselves – perhaps too much time?

11. IF JAPANESE COMPANIES REALLY WANT TO BE GLOBAL, THEIR WORKERS NEED MORE FLEXIBILITY

Many creative ideas were proposed in Japan to deal with the power shortages after the Fukushima earthquake in 2011, such as making Friday a holiday and working on Saturday instead. The more articles I read describing these ideas, the more I hoped that flexible working will finally take off in Japan.

It's been long overdue and much discussed as one way of encouraging women to re-join the workforce. But I have always thought that unless a critical mass of Japanese companies decides to adopt it – in the face of some overriding social need – rather than a token gesture towards diversity in the workplace aimed at women only – it will never happen in a widespread way.

Being able to work from home has an obvious advantage in a power crisis – it creates less of a burden on the energy hungry national transport system. It also enables more resilience should, heaven forbid, another major earthquake strike Japan, as workers will be more dispersed rather than concentrated in one vulnerable office building.

The long-term benefits to society, other than the obvious one of allowing more women to return to work, would be that presenteeism – staying long hours in the office to prove loyalty to the team and the company – might finally stop being the norm. It's hard for Japanese companies to accept that presenteeism has come to a natural end, because one of the fundamental attitudes behind overtime is group orientation. You have never finished your work for the day, because you could always be helping someone else in your team.

One of the major changes in the British workplace over the past decade or so has been the increase in what I call "grey zone" working – thanks to smartphones, we can check our work e-mails during the morning and evening commute.

Lightweight laptops and the ability to log on remotely to corporate servers mean we can easily take our work home with us. This worries Japanese companies, who see all the security risks that entails. But now they also realise that there are security risks in having data concentrated in hardware in one location.

One of the other reasons the UK has taken to flexible working is the fact that we are in an ideal location in terms of time zones. We can pick up from Asia in the morning, and "baton touch" as the Japanese say, to our colleagues in North America in the afternoon. Early morning and late evening phone calls are much more bearable if we can do them from home.

Of course, we also realise we have to keep a balance in terms of social interaction and knowledge sharing with our colleagues. A whole week at home would not help us do our jobs properly either. I hope Japan can bridge the gap at the other end of the world's day, from North America on to Europe via Asia, but it will take flexible working hours to make that a reality.

12. AU PAIRS FOR JAPAN?

Autumn is the start of the new academic year across Europe. Parents rush around trying to make sure all the right pieces of clothing, stationery and sports gear have been purchased and labelled. At the same time, working parents have to deal with a sudden burst of activity at work, as customers wake up after the long summer holidays.

We had seven au pairs over a period of six years. Without the assistance of our au pairs taking our son to school, helping him with his homework, cleaning the house and being available for babysitting, my husband and I would not have been able to cope with both our jobs and looking after our son.

Most of our au pairs have been German - it is easiest to hire au pairs who come from one of the European Union countries because there are no visa problems or worries about illegal workers. We are fortunate that because we are based in the UK, we have many candidates to choose from, as most au pairs want to learn English. Usually au pairs are around eighteen years old, and want to take a year before university to experience another country and culture and give themselves more time to choose which university and which course they want to apply for.

As well as being a help to parents, I also like the fact that my son gets used to communicating with people who are a different nationality to him, so he is aware of other cultures and ways of behaving.

I wonder whether the Japanese government, in its quest for Japan to become more global in outlook, particularly with the 2020 Olympics in mind, might consider a similar au pair scheme. I realise that many

Japanese homes are too small to accommodate another person. But I remember very fondly the year I spent with a Japanese family in Hiroshima when I was 18. They had to move their son and daughter into the same bedroom to free up a room for me, which was not very popular with their children, but I think overall, they felt everyone benefitted from having a foreigner as a temporary member of the family.

The mother did not work, apart from some occasional English language teaching, so I did not have to do much to help around the house. Instead of the family paying me an allowance (we pay our au pair £75 a week), my parents paid some money to the family for my upkeep.

However, if Japan were to introduce an au pair scheme, I would expect the other benefit to be that Japanese mothers would feel more able to re-join the workplace, with the peace of mind that their children and house were being looked after. This would also support another objective of the government, to get more women back to work by improving childcare.

13. SUBTLE FACTORS THAT MOTIVATE WORKERS DIFFER IN JAPAN AND WEST

Every time a Japanese company acquires a Western company, there is a concern about how the Japanese organization will deal with the "high risk, high reward" culture that is prevalent not only in the financial industry but across many Western business sectors.

Actually, Japanese multinationals have been dealing with this issue for some years, and the solution has usually been to pay the local market rate. It does, of course, result in some anomalies. Presidents of Japanese blue-chip companies are paid only around 10-20 times the salary of the lowest paid worker, whereas a Fortune 500 CEO can earn anywhere from 300-500 times a junior employee's salary.

So, it may turn out that the Japanese president is earning significantly less than the foreign directors reporting to him from the acquired company. Lower down the ranks, more junior Japanese find that when they are posted overseas, they are having to manage locally hired hotshots who are earning salaries and bonuses that add up to the equivalent of an extra zero on the end of a normal Japanese expat salary.

Many Japanese working for foreign banks and consultancies in Japan have also been making 10 times the average salary in Japan. Of course, Japanese on traditional salary packages can comfort themselves with the thought that they have more secure jobs, especially given what has been happened since the Lehman Shock. But I think there is a danger in oversimplifying this risk/reward trade-off.

Knowing that you won't be laid off when times get tough, or conversely that you are being paid handsomely, is not sufficient for most people, Japanese or Western, to feel completely fulfilled and motivated in their work. These factors may ensure people stay in their jobs but not that they perform those jobs to the best of their abilities.

High salaries and bonuses are in some ways proxies for the things that really motivate people to work. Being paid well should indicate that an employee is doing something that has had a major impact on the company. It should also reflect the employee's authority and responsibility to make an impact. Getting quick raises should show that one's career is advancing and that one's skills and capabilities are developing.

These are all drivers of engagement – pride and motivation in work – for people working in Western companies. Surveys show that the drivers of engagement for Japanese people working in Japanese companies are subtly different. Career advancement opportunities and ability to make an impact are important, but so are other factors – immediate personal relationships, having input to department decisions, and having a manager who understands what motivates each employee and who has good relationships with them.

All people, regardless of nationality, want to feel recognized for making a positive difference in the world through their work. For many Japanese, the traditional way to do this has been through becoming a long time respected member of a major company. For many Westerners, this route does not exist, so impact on society has to be more visibly rewarded through pay or status.

Japanese and Western companies need to avoid two extremes when trying to combine corporate cultures. Paying people well but not giving them the authority to make an impact and advance their careers will eventually lead Westerners to leave a company. Offering lifetime employment but without good, enduring personal relationships and mutual respect may mean that although Japanese employees stay, their morale is low.

14. PROFESSIONAL STATUS AS AN ALTERNATIVE TO PROMOTION

After the Lehman Shock hit, I asked one of the two partners of a local firm of accountants whether he was getting lots of job applications from recently made redundant accountants from the big accounting firms. He said he was, but he had to be careful about hiring such people as his firm cannot offer the career path that the big firms can. "People who are used to big companies get frustrated and quit when they realise there is not much potential for meaningful promotion with us," he said.

It reminded me of the situation I often see in Japanese companies in Europe. Partly because of the fragmented nature of Europe, unlike the USA, many Japanese companies find the best structure is to have a small office in each country with one or two expatriate Japanese staff in each one. The locally hired staff often have interesting and varied jobs because the small office has to cover a variety of functions and businesses. However, there is not much of a vertical structure in terms of people for them to "manage" if they are promoted to a management position.

How, then, should such Japanese companies retain and motivate good quality local staff? The accountancy firm partner said what he did was offer good salaries, excellent benefits and plenty of training. This may not be sufficient to satisfy ambitious people, however, so I have a couple of other suggestions specifically for Japanese companies in Europe.

One is to try to create a pan-European structure so that locally hired staff can have some status within that structure, not just their local one. It may not be possible to have actual job roles like "European Sales Director" but a human network could be created, through pan European meetings and training. Then people can keep in touch afterwards by using an intranet to put their profiles on and exchange information through blogs or wikis. Through getting to know each other and sharing expertise, the high-flying staff will begin to gain unofficial status and recognition. People might also become less reluctant about the idea of moving to another location or to take on a "pan European" role, once they know more about other colleagues in other European operations and what they do.

The other way Japanese companies can motivate their ambitious staff is to give them opportunities to improve their status within their profession. This might not seem to the Japanese management as being much of an issue. Many Japanese employees feel they have enough status professionally because their company is so well known and respected in Japan. But often such companies are not at all famous outside of Japan. The kind of opportunities I have in mind are, for example, joining professional associations, gaining professional qualifications, speaking at conferences, writing articles for trade journals etc.

If Japanese companies can support their locally hired staff in gaining recognition and respect inside and outside their companies, they may have more success in retaining motivated, ambitious employees.

15. OVERSEAS EXPERIENCE AND JAPAN'S ELITE, PAST AND PRESENT

When I started working at Mitsubishi Corporation in London, I was intrigued by the fact that Mitsubishi had first opened the office there as early as 1915. Most British people, if they have thought about it at all, would assume Japanese companies did not establish themselves in the UK until well after World War Two. In fact, it turned out Mitsubishi Corporation was a relative late comer to London amongst the *sogo shosha* (Japanese trading companies), although the Iwasaki founding family had links with the UK from long before 1915.

I was reminded of these links thanks to a recent talk by Dr Ohnuma Shinichi, professor of Experimental Ophthalmology at University College London (UCL) to Japanese business people in London, where he showed slide after slide of the names of the Japanese future elite who studied at UCL in the Meiji era, starting with the 14 students from the Satsuma clan in 1865, through to Iwasaki Toshiya, who studied Chemistry at UCL in 1901.

Dr Ohnuma was showing us these slides to remind us of how the founders of the modern Japanese state and business had fearlessly travelled and lived abroad, and there was a keen discussion afterwards as to how this spirit of adventure could be revived amongst young Japanese people now.

One of Dr Ohnuma's suggestions was that Japanese companies should demonstrate that there is a positive advantage to have worked abroad, and to ensure there are proper roles for their employees with overseas experience to fulfil when they return.

At Mitsubishi Corporation it was an unwritten rule that top executives have overseas experience, and as a consequence, most new graduates join Mitsubishi Corporation and other trading companies in the expectation that they will be posted abroad. I realise however, that for other major Japanese companies, whose origins are more domestically oriented, it would be rather hard to implement this rule straight away, when in most cases hardly any of their current executives have overseas experience.

Smaller companies may have more scope to put such criteria in place however. The leaders of such companies can set the tone themselves, just as Sony's Morita Akio did in 1963, when he controversially relocated himself and his family to New York, in order to understand the US market better.

It is surely no coincidence that the former President of Sony, Hirai Kazuo, lived abroad as a child and worked for Sony overseas. Despite Naruke Makoto (ex President of Microsoft Japan)'s assertion that nobody has ever succeeded who went to international school, Hirai did indeed go to the American School in Tokyo.

Sony may have had its problems, but it seems to have succeeded in its revival plans, and proves that the spirit of entrepreneurism, openness to the world outside Japan and adaptability to change of its founder can live on, if the founder himself has set the tone correctly by his own actions.

16. COPING WITH AN AGEING WORKFORCE

I visited Japan for the first time in a year and a half in December 2013. I try to go to Japan once a year, each time looking out for subtle changes in a country I have been visiting or living in for the past forty years.

This time I felt some of the *"genki"* (a useful Japanese word meaning energy and health) had come back, compared to visits in 2011 and 2012 when there seemed to be a general atmosphere of depression.

However, I also felt Tokyo had slowed down. There were visibly more elderly people, but also the younger people moved more slowly, partly as they were gazing into their smartphones as they walked.

Japan's *"yasashisa"* (gentleness) and rich cultural life make it a great place to grow old. Of course I realise that it is the current generation of retirees who have it the best − a decent pension and healthier, longer lives in which to enjoy it.

My generation, both in Japan and many European countries, face the prospect of not being able to retire until we are 70. So we have at least another 20 years of working life ahead of us. In Europe it is now illegal for employers to discriminate on the grounds of age, and the default retirement age of 65 has been phased out in the UK.

Europeans reaching their fifties will not be able to afford to retire early as previously. But if they cling on to their jobs they are made to feel like they are blocking the way for younger people and are vulnerable to redundancy programmes.

It is hard to get a job in another company once you are over fifty − and there is also a question of motivation. The prospect of another 20 years doing the same thing − particularly if it is a *"gemba"* (shop floor) type, active, high pressure job, is not appealing. The second half of a working life should be more about reflecting on acquired knowledge and skills and handing them on to the next generation.

I'm not sure the initiatives taken in Japan since the 1990s to deal with this − such as *kata tataki* (literally "shoulder tapping" where employees in their late 40s are forcefully offered very early retirement) and *madogiwazoku* (the window tribe − people who have been given a seat by the window and no real job to do) really worked. It was not only disheartening for those directly impacted, but also for the younger generation, who have reacted by becoming more risk averse. They want lifetime employment, but don't see the point of being ambitious or taking risks such as working abroad.

A better way might be to help people in the second half of their working life find ways of capturing their accumulated knowledge and skills and transmitting them to the younger generation in Japan – through teaching rather than as a manager.

Locally hired employees and managers in overseas acquisitions would also welcome having an appointed mentor to help them feel more connected to Japan headquarters and understand the corporate culture and processes. If Japan could refresh its traditions of *sempai/kōhai* (mentoring of juniors by seniors) and apprenticeship for the 21st century, I believe it could be a pioneer in developing a humane but productive ageing society.

Pernille Rudlin

CHAPTER 3
HOW TO BE A GOOD CORPORATE CITIZEN IN EUROPE

1. THE NEED FOR PR BEYOND PRESS RELEASES

30 years ago, I became one of the first ever graduate trainees at the London office of the US public relations consultancy Burson Marsteller. Burson Marsteller told me they were starting various joint ventures with Dentsu in Europe, so it seemed like a great opportunity to use my interest in Japan and my communication skills to support Japanese companies who had been arriving in Europe in increasing numbers in the past decade.

PR in Europe at the time was mostly staffed by ex-journalists, focused on producing press releases, and wining and dining journalist contacts so they would write favourably about clients. Changes were in the air, however, which is why major PR consultancies like Burson Marsteller were starting to hire and train new graduates to be "communications professionals".

In the late Eighties, the Big Bang revolutionised the City of London's investment banks and stock market, and nationalised industries were being privatised. I was assigned to a corporate PR team, looking after British Gas (which later became Centrica) and a building society, which was thinking of floating on the stock exchange.

They were both facing the new pressures on companies to communicate to stakeholders. Not just to their new shareholders, but also to the communities in which they operated. They needed to show they could still be trusted, even if they weren't owned by the state, or by account holders. There was also a need to polish their reputation so they could attract high potential graduates.

Japanese companies in Europe have the same needs – now as they did then – but unfortunately I do not think much progress has been made these past 30 years. There are so many companies which are famous in Japan but are either utterly unknown in Europe, or the name is familiar, but there is no notion of what they do, or whether they are good corporate citizens.

Nothing came of the Dentsu joint venture thirty years ago, but I see now that Dentsu itself has started acquiring companies in Europe and other Japanese PR and advertising companies are strengthening their presence here.

Not only do Japanese companies have foreign shareholders to keep happy, but if they are to succeed in overseas social infrastructure projects, they must ensure that the communities affected are informed and welcoming, and that the best overseas graduates view them as a prestigious place to work.

This is not just a Japanese problem – I once participated in a survey which I assume was commissioned by Siemens. The survey asked whether I knew that Siemens had been in the UK since 1843, was one of the largest graduate employers in the UK, with 12 factories, and involved with all kinds of sustainable energy and infrastructure projects. I was ashamed of my own ignorance of this, but amused to see that one of the competitors they were benchmarking themselves against was my old client, Centrica.

2. NETWORKING AND REPUTATION

In common with many Japanese businesses at the end of the financial year (which is usually March 31st in Japan), I not only review budgets, but also which memberships of chambers of commerce and similar organisations to renew.

Most European businesses, if asked to justify membership of such organisations, would say it is for the networking, to meet potential business leads. Indeed, the London Chamber of Commerce, of which my company was a member, emphasises this most of all when promoting itself. However, I never went to any of their networking events because not many companies in my target market - Japanese businesses - are members.

My main reason for being a member of the London Chamber of Commerce was that they have excellent meeting rooms in central London where I can hold my seminars, and there is a discount for members, which just about covers the cost of the membership and even saves money if you hold enough seminars in one year.

The other two reasons the London Chamber uses to promote membership are the support services it provides – mainly HR, legal and export trade related – and that it acts as a voice for businesses in London, and will lobby government on our behalf.

I also belong to the Japanese Chamber of Commerce and Industry in the UK. In fact, my company was the first company without a Japanese headquarters or subsidiary to become a member, following a change in the rules. The rules were changed because membership was declining – I suspect because during the 1990s Japanese companies were cutting costs wherever they could.

Membership has recovered since – with record numbers attending recent New Year's parties. This was probably a sign of the recovering Japanese and UK economies, and also that thanks to the increasingly strict immigration laws in the UK, the Japanese Chamber of Commerce has an important role for its members in lobbying the British government.

At most of the chamber's networking events, however, I find myself exchanging business cards with British professional services companies like mine, which is somewhat pointless, as we are all more interested in meeting potential Japanese customers, than each other.

It's difficult to claim that any of the fifty or so Japanese clients I now have were as a direct result of meetings at such events. However, I can still justify the membership cost because of the membership directory, which not only gives me contact and addresses, but provides up to date information on the reorganisations and relocations of Japanese companies in Europe.

There is one further reason for continuing to be a member – reputation. It shows other members you are serious about the business community you belong to, and are a respectable organisation. In fact, in France and Germany it is obligatory to be a member of a chamber of commerce if you set up a business there. The Japanese Chamber of Commerce in the UK is also aware of its ability to confer respectability – the main concern they had when I first applied to join was to ensure I was not running a dating agency!

3. HIGH BRAND RECOGNITION DOES NOT MEAN YOU ARE WELL KNOWN

When it was first suggested to me that I join Mitsubishi Corporation in the UK, I have to admit I thought it was the car manufacturer, Mitsubishi Motors, despite the fact that I should have known better, having been brought up in Japan and spent a year at a Japanese university.

After a couple of years exporting British chinaware and shoes to Japan for the trading house, I was transferred to Tokyo to work in the building materials sales team. The apartment that my employer found for me had no furniture, as is normal in Japan. So I decided I would buy what I needed at Marui department store, as I had heard they offered credit cards and I did not have enough savings to pay for the necessary bed, sofa and refrigerator.

When I approached the credit card application desk, a look of panic flitted across the clerk's face – a young, foreign, female was presumably not going to be a good credit risk. I reassured him I could speak Japanese, but he was very concerned whether I could write well enough to fill in the application form.

I took out my Mitsubishi Corporation business card in order to copy down the address, and as soon as he spotted the distinctive three diamond logo, his face lit up. "Mitsubishi Corporation! Can I phone your team leader to check your employment details?" He returned from the call with a huge smile on his face, and tried to make me buy two televisions and a better refrigerator.

The Mitsubishi name worked magic for me once more in my career there. I had stupidly forgotten my passport on a trip to Frankfurt from London. The German border police were not impressed, particularly as I had no other form of ID, not even a driving license or credit card. I suddenly remembered my Mitsubishi security pass.

Again, the atmosphere improved dramatically, and one policeman even tried to make a joke of it – "we will let you through, if you can get us a Shogun!" (as the Pajero sport utility vehicle was known in Europe at the time).

I decided this was not a good moment to explain that Mitsubishi Corporation was not the same company as Mitsubishi Motors, and ruefully remembered how I had made the same mistake myself a few years previously in the job interview. In retrospect, it is intriguing that the Mitsubishi brand instantly evoked trust, even for a German policeman who did not really know what it stood for.

This was twenty years ago, but I suspect this paradox persists for Japanese companies when it comes to recruiting in Europe. There is a generally favourable view of Japanese companies, but nobody is quite sure what they do, and therefore there is a doubt as to whether becoming an employee of a Japanese company is a good career move.

It's no surprise, therefore, that the larger Japanese employers in Europe are indeed putting more effort into broader corporate communications, rather than just product advertising. This is presumably in order to attract the best quality employees.

4. EUROPE'S LOSS OF CONFIDENCE IN THE FOOD SUPPLY CHAIN - CAN JAPAN STEP UP?

I used to be able to horrify my British friends by telling them that I have eaten *bazashi* (horse sashimi) in Japan – they could not believe that I would happily eat horse, and eat it raw. British reactions, however, to the discovery in 2013 that many readymade burgers and lasagne bought in supermarkets contain horsemeat rather than 100% beef was more about the fear of not knowing what is in our food, rather than disgust at the idea of having inadvertently eaten horse.

Although we don't eat horse meat in the UK, we are aware that many of our European neighbours do, and are not as repulsed by the idea as we used to be. What we find really troubling this time is that the supply chains for the food we buy have become so complex that we cannot be sure exactly what the ingredients are and where they have come from.

The British middle classes have become far more interested in good quality, locally sourced food this past decade. Our TV schedules are full of cookery programmes – not quite as many as Japan perhaps – and our restaurants have improved tremendously. Italians and French are famously obsessed by the seasonality and quality of food – but they too have been affected by the horsemeat contamination scandal. In fact, the supply chains involved in the scandal seem to go through almost every country in the EU, from the Netherlands to Romania.

Many commentators lay the blame on lower income consumers' desire to buy food as cheaply as possible, particularly in the current economic climate. The fierce price competition between supermarkets has led to pressures being applied right through the supply chain, and corners being cut in terms of quality checks. Supermarkets have, rightly, refrained from defending themselves by saying they were only trying to provide what consumers want or by blaming suppliers. They realise even the poorest consumer is placing trust in their brand, and does not want to be tricked. So they are taking steps to cut out middlemen between them and the farmers, or to bring meat processing back in house.

Some commentators have pointed out that there are parallels with the US car industry in the 1980s. American car firms were competing on price, so forced their suppliers to cut prices, with a consequent drop in quality. This enabled Japanese car firms, who worked far more collaboratively with their suppliers, to produce high quality vehicles, at reasonable prices, to take market share.

When Japanese car companies entered Europe, they made sure their supply chain followed them in setting up in Europe, or that local suppliers worked as closely with them as their suppliers would in Japan. Japanese car companies have recognised the importance of the brand – it is not just promoting a logo, but whole ethos of responsibility to the customer.

Notably, when there are quality problems, Japanese car firms act as the public face to the customer, apologising and implementing product recalls. The root cause may be a supplier defect, but the supplier is not publicly named. The brand owner takes responsibility for the whole supply chain, and customers do not want to hear the blame being pushed onto someone else.

Japan has had its own food contamination scandals, but on balance, I believe Japanese companies manage their supply chains very well. The test will be how the next wave of Japanese companies in customer facing industries such as retail, airlines and food, who are trying to become global brands, and often buy up European brands in order to do so, will be able to replicate their trusted supply chains successfully in Europe. The beef contamination scandal has put European customers on the alert.

5. NETHERLANDS AND CORPORATE TAXES

The choice of the Netherlands for Panasonic's new financial and tax base for its pan-European business, to be shifted out of the UK in October 2018 to prepare for Brexit, comes as no surprise – even though most of Panasonic's regional business coordination is in Germany. In fact, I even predicted Amsterdam would be a top choice for Japanese companies in 2013 when Brexit proofing strategies were first being discussed.

The Netherlands has a relatively high density of Japanese company transferees, 4th in Europe after Luxembourg, UK and Belgium. This population has been expanding rapidly since 2015 too – there are 23% more Japanese people on company transfers in 2017 compared to 2015. The number of Japanese companies in the Netherlands has not risen much over the three years, however. So most of these transfers will have been in order to strengthen presence there, rather than start up a new operation.

The attractions of the Netherlands as an alternative to the UK over Germany are not only that is easy to function in English, but also that Amsterdam/Amstelveen area has long had a good infrastructure of networking opportunities with an active Japanese Chamber of Commerce and the Dutch & Japanese Trade Federation. There are also plenty of lawyers and financial services providers with experience of supporting Japanese companies. The Amsterdam lifestyle is congenial, and there is a history of over 500 years of trade relations with Japan.

Panasonic Europe's French CEO Laurent Abadie gave Japan's new tax haven laws as one other factor in the decision, besides concerns over the loss of freedom of movement of people, goods and capital if the UK leaves the EU single market without any compensating agreement.

This point was lost in the fuss that ensued from Abadie's Brexit related remarks, but upon further investigation, I realise that it is indeed something that Japanese companies have to take into consideration.

My understanding is that from April 2018, Japanese companies with subsidiaries overseas that act as holding companies for other foreign subsidiaries may find that dividends and other passive income will be subject to Japanese tax – even if the holding company has substantial presence and business activities – if the host country has an effective corporate tax rate below 20%.

Even before the Brexit referendum, the UK government had committed to progressively reducing corporation tax, to 19% in 2019 and then 18% from 2020. The 2020 rate was then reduced even further to 17%, and the current Chancellor of the Exchequer has pledged to stick with this, to show that Britain is "open for business", despite Brexit.

The corporate tax rate in the Netherlands is 25%, although it is well known that the Dutch tax authorities are open to deals with multinationals to reduce the effective rate to well below this.

British companies were not very welcoming of the reduction in UK corporation tax to 17%. Like Panasonic, they would rather have barrier free trade and globally agreed, transparent governance standards.

6. WHY IS THERE NO WORD FOR RISK IN JAPANESE?

Listening to the presentation of Yoshida Kazumasa, the CEO of Emergency Assistance Japan a couple of years' ago, I was yet again struck by the fact that there is no direct translation in Japanese for the English word "risk". Yoshida even had a slide to define "risk", with "risk" written as "リスク"(risuku) in the *katakana* alphabet, implying that it is a borrowed word. His definition of risk was the potential for a crisis to occur, which if then becomes reality, is a threat, and then when there is harm, is a crisis.

"危機"(kiki) is sometimes used instead of "risuku". This causes problems when trying to distinguish between risk management and crisis management in Japanese. Risk management becomes two borrowed foreign words "リスク・マネジメント"(risuku manejimento) and crisis management is the entirely Japanese "危機管理"(kiki kanri).

I asked Yoshida why there was no word for risk in Japanese. He said it was indeed puzzling, when you considered how prone to natural disasters Japan was. His view was that it was something in the Japanese mind-set, that cannot deal with a crisis in advance, only if it happens in front of their eyes. This, he added, is why Japan has not coped so well in terms of preventing natural disasters from turning into wider crises, as with the Fukushima earthquake.

Most humans are bad at assessing and dealing with risk, vastly overestimating the probability of facing situations they cannot personally control (airplane crashes, terrorist attacks) and vastly underestimating the risk posed to them by situations they think they can control, such as crossing the road, or skiing. So it's the very fact that Japan has had a history of massive and regular natural disasters such as earthquakes, volcanoes and tsunami, that causes a numbness to set in. The Japanese expression "carp on a chopping board" springs to mind, where the carp becomes calm when faced with a chopping board and a knife, hoping for an easy death.

A lot of effort is put into preventing the crisis from happening in the first place, rather than putting a plan in place to deal with inevitable risks. When a crisis does happen, it is usually covered up rather than dealt with, and Japanese companies are riddled with processes for double and triple checking, imposed after a mistake has happened.

Yoshida had a clear recommendation for what Japanese companies should do, namely, appoint an executive to be responsible for "risk". They should not be someone who has been moved horizontally away from business line management because they are deemed to be no longer effective (a practice known as yoko suberi in Japanese). They need to have the ear of the President and be able command business units on what they should do. It should therefore be an important and recognised role – either for a specialist, or be made as a precondition that any President should have occupied the role. And they should be someone who, as Yoshida put it, "doesn't run away." In this increasingly risky and uncertain world, it's time Japanese companies had a global risk translator.

7. JAPANESE COMPANIES NEED TO BE MORE PROACTIVE IN THEIR CSR

Many of our Japanese clients in Europe have become active in Turkey over the past decade, so when I heard the Association of Japanese Business Studies annual conference was going to be in Istanbul in 2013, I decided to combine attendance at the conference with meeting potential partners and business contacts.

Other conference attendees did not seem aware of this renewed interest in Turkey by Japanese companies, but the Turkish businesspeople I spoke to certainly were. In fact, one of my Turkish business friends was quick to ask me how Turkish people should react to the news that a Japanese consortium will be building Turkey's third nuclear power station.

My Turkish friend also described the Gezi Park protests to me as a welcome revival in political activism by the younger generation. This comment, and his question regarding the nuclear power project made me wonder whether Japanese companies are fully aware of how much they might be under the spotlight, as they become more involved in infrastructure projects across Europe and the Middle East.

Japanese companies' reputations as corporate citizens will be vital in terms of being able to hire good people, gain acceptance in the community and win support from governments and other business partners.

It's not that Japanese companies are bad corporate citizens – quite the opposite in fact – but more that they continue to be modest in communicating about what they do, or are unaware that they do not have as strong a reputation outside of Japan as they do domestically.

One paper at the conference was regarding the Corporate Social Responsibility activities of Japanese pharmaceutical companies. The presenter concluded that whilst Japanese companies were careful to comply with regulations in other countries, they were not very proactive in promoting global CSR initiatives (other than issuing annual CSR reports) – for example the campaign to ensure poorer countries have access to medicines.

They also tend to be passive participants in global standards and evaluations, which – admittedly – are largely driven by US originated criteria.

This reminded me of a conversation I had a few weeks previously with the CSR manager in a Japanese-owned food company in the UK. He had been a sales manager previously and had moved to CSR because of the increasing frustration he was feeling in sales meetings with British supermarkets. "It's no longer enough to show our ingredients are responsibly sourced and meet various certification standards. The supermarkets want to know what we are actually doing ourselves to promote sustainability".

Japanese companies who want to meet this challenge will have to reframe their visions and values in ways that make them more actionable and less vague. This should be an integral part of employee development, so that employees have a reference point for their actions and can talk knowledgeably to customers and partners about how the company is contributing to the societies in which it operates. They need to be clear what the company stands for, and what it is doing about it.

8. THE POSITIVES AND NEGATIVES FOR INVESTORS OF LOCAL PRIDE AND IDENTITY

I was working in Catalonia just before the referendum there in 2017 and shortly after that I was in the North Rhine-Westphalia area in Germany, just after the German elections. These trips, as well as the impact of Brexit in the UK, made me aware of how important local – not just national – identities are for businesses to thrive.

The majority of Japanese companies based in Spain are in the Catalonia region, and this choice of location is not surprising as Catalonia has been one of the most prosperous and industrialized areas of the country, offering easy land access to France and several international ports. It turns out that one of the factors behind the Catalan independence movement is a resentment amongst the people of the region that their taxes are being transferred to prop up poorer parts of Spain.

The freedom of capital, labour, goods and services in the European single market creates competition between not just countries but also regions within those countries to attract investment from business. The European Union tries to prevent this turning into a "race to the bottom" in terms of cost of labour, tax rates and cost of capital by having tough regulations on labour standards, cracking down on tax avoidance and limiting how far member governments can subsidise business investment.

Before 2008 the system seemed to work well – labour flowed to the more prosperous parts of the EU where there were job shortages and capital flowed from those regions (and from Japan) to regions where the cost of labour was lower.

In a free market, this should have eventually led to an equalization of living standards across the European Union. However, the Lehman Shock, combined with the influx of new member countries from Eastern Europe meant that capital flows returned to the safer havens of Western and Northern Europe and workers in southern and eastern Europe left their home towns to find work elsewhere in greater numbers than before.

The tension this caused is particularly apparent in Germany. The anti-immigrant Alternativ für Deutschland had very little support in the 2017 elections in the prosperous North Rhine-Westphalia region – which has one the highest concentration of Japanese companies in Europe. But it had strong support in former communist eastern Germany, where the continuing gap in living standards with the west causes resentment, fuelled by worries that immigrants from other eastern European countries are further eroding wages.

For Japanese companies considering investment in Europe, local sensitivities add another layer of complexity in choosing a company to acquire or a locational base. However, if Japanese companies show strong local commitment, the local employees will respond with equal loyalty and commitment too. This is very clear in the pride and loyalty of employees at Japanese automotive plants which have been operating for over 25 years in some of most deprived parts of the UK, who have expressed their determination to succeed despite Brexit.

9. WHAT I HAVE LEARNT FROM AIRBNB ABOUT HOW TO MANAGE A MULTINATIONAL BUSINESS

There was a backlash in summer 2017 in Europe against Airbnb and more widely against the impact of tourism on cities such as Venice and Barcelona. With the new *minpaku* (private residents taking lodgers) law being enacted in Japan, and Japan having its own tourism boom, there is much to learn for Japan and Europe from the "sharing economy" and its impact not just on the tourism industry but communities and global business.

I have used Airbnb both as a guest and also to rent out our spare room. All our guests have been friendly, tidy and responsible and have ranged from a Pakistani PhD student through to a comedian duo from Canada. My initial concerns about allowing strangers into our home have not been justified.

Airbnb helps with this by verifying identities – of host and guest – and encouraging people to upload personal details such as photos of themselves, their interests and the reason for their visit. Airbnb also provides a very user-friendly platform and plenty of support and advice to enable good communication and high standards of behaviour and facilities.

What is becoming clear, however, is that Airbnb has a lot more work to do at the local level. As disruptive companies mature, their business becomes more mainstream. There are more and more professional holiday letting companies appearing on Airbnb and whole houses and apartments – not just spare rooms – can be booked via the site. This is raising concerns about whether the appropriate taxes are being paid, whether the accommodation is sufficiently regulated in terms of safety and potential nuisance to neighbours and whether the bigger profits to be gained from putting properties on Airbnb rather than traditional renting is exacerbating housing shortages for local residents.

Theories of how to manage multinational businesses tend to focus on balancing local and global needs – for example the matrix structure of vertical businesses and horizontal functions, or making sure that brands are "glocal" – globally recognisable but with a local flavour – like a McDonald's teriyaki burger.

What I have learnt from Airbnb is that the "personal" is also important. You need to be able to verify, trust and feel empathy with the customer/guest or supplier/host as a person, even if they come from a different culture to you.

Japanese multinationals are usually quite good at the local aspect – they pay their taxes and are good corporate citizens. At the global level, Japanese car brands in particular are making the transition towards becoming a "platform" – they provide the globally assured brand, design and quality standards in assembling parts from multiple regional suppliers.

The next challenge is the personal level. Japanese executives are self-effacing (mostly) and Japanese social media users prefer to stay anonymous and not reveal which companies they work for. But in order to ensure your company is "verifiable" and "trusted" by your customers, it will be necessary for the local face of your company to be more personal.

10. GDPR

The EU's General Data Protection Regulation (GDPR) came into force on May 25th 2018 – after which date, organizations which hold personal data on EU citizens which are not compliant with the GDPR may face heavy fines.

Many small companies like mine struggled to comply. The regulation is clearly aimed at the larger business-to-consumer companies who hold a lot of very personal data about their customers, such as their age, sexuality, political affiliations and so on, and could use this to target them in a way that could be seen as intrusive or offensive.

I decided, however, to make sure the personal data we hold is compliant, partly because I want my customers to feel confident that their suppliers are trustworthy, but also because I see this as a chance to improve the service we provide and slim down our customer database and mailing lists.

Japanese companies in Europe are undoubtedly feeling particularly nervous about the GDPR, as Honda Motor Europe was already fined by the UK's Information Commissioner's Office in 2017 for violating a UK regulation which has very similar requirements to the GDPR regarding consent.

Consent is the key issue with GDPR. There needs to be informed, positive consent by the customer for their data to be processed. The nature of the data (what kind of personal details) the company will hold, and what it will be used for (emails, newsletters, postal mailing etc) have to be clearly explained. A double opt in is recommended – whereby people fill in the form, and then receive an email asking them to confirm that they do want to share their data. A clear process for them to ask to be deleted from a database also needs to be in place.

It is not possible to "grandfather" (allow old conditions to continue even if they are against the new rules) previously held personal data, so it is safest to reconfirm with people on your database that they still consent to you processing their data. Of course, the risk with this is that many people will not consent and your mailing list will shrink.

But this brings me on to my second reason for deciding to comply as thoroughly as possible with the GDPR. I want to make sure that my newsletters are really valued by my customers. Our newsletters are not marketing our training so much as part of the after-service we provide. They help our customers refresh and add to what they learnt in the classroom.

Manufacturers are also moving away from just selling a product, to selling a solution – hardware plus surrounding services such as maintenance and support, using the Internet of Things and Big Data to provide a more customised product.

Which is of course why the GDPR has become necessary. Personal data can be used in a good way, to meet customer needs more completely, but, as we know in Europe, particularly in former dictatorships and communist regimes, personal data can be abused.

11. DOES IT HELP JAPANESE COMPANIES TO GLOBALIZE IF THERE ARE MORE WOMEN MANAGERS?

I attended a dinner in 2014 hosted by a delegation to the UK from J-WIN (Japan Women's Innovative Network, a non-profit organisation) where the question of whether having more women managers would help Japanese companies to globalise was raised, but not discussed in depth due to time constraints.

An impressively large number of younger Japanese women (70) had been sponsored by their companies to come to the UK for a week, visiting various UK companies such as British Telecom and Aon Insurance, to study global leadership and diversity.

My view is yes, it does help Japanese companies to globalise if they have more (Japanese) women managers, for a couple of reasons. Firstly, it helps Japanese companies and corporate culture seem less "alien" to Western companies if there are more women in management positions in the headquarters, and secondly, because the adjustments Japanese companies will have to make in order to incorporate a more diverse Japanese workforce will help them be more inclusive of "non-Japanese" diverse groups. Attitudes to overtime and working from home would be a couple of areas needing adjustment I would suggest.

Most companies in Europe allow much more flexible working than was accepted even ten years ago. Men have taken advantage of these new ways of working too – one senior British male manager I know works from home at least three days a week so that he can take his children to and from school. It helps that many senior global jobs involve communicating by phone or web conferences and email, managing dispersed teams, which can be done from anywhere, at any time.

Many Japanese companies have announced targets for percentages of women in management positions. Some European countries such as Norway have taken this a step further by putting regulations in place to enforce quotas of how many women should be on the boards of listed companies. However, many companies resist imposing quotas, fearing that it will only isolate women further if they are seen to have been promoted merely because of their gender rather than ability.

Instead of quotas, many European companies have set up mentoring schemes, to encourage men to network with and promote women. This is something that I think Japanese companies can benefit from adopting, not just for women, but for their non-Japanese employees, by using the existing *sempai/kōhai* (senior/junior) concept. Mentoring in a Western sense tends to be very focused on developing the mentee's career. I like the more all-encompassing *sempai/kōhai* relationship, which is informal, and more about accessing each other's networks across the company, to help the mentee feel "part of the family".

I talked about mentoring with a couple of the J-WIN women. One, from a *gaishi* (foreign owned firm in Japan), said she found being mentored by an American man far more effective than being mentored by a Japanese man, as the American mentor had no preconceptions about Japanese women's roles and behaviour. I suspect non-Japanese employees will find it equally helpful to have a mentor who can explain Japanese corporate culture from the inside.

12. DIVERSITY ON BOARDS

The UK business media paid more attention than usual to Japanese business topics in 2015, thanks to the new corporate governance regulations that were introduced in Japan that year. Corporate governance is still a hot topic in the UK, more than 25 years on from the Cadbury Report which made similar recommendations to those being adopted in Japan, and has been influential on EU and US regulations since.

External directors are now a standard feature of British boards, but there is still concern that there is a lack of diversity in the membership of the boards of British companies. What we call in the UK an "Old Boys' Network" still operates in the appointment of board members. It is a natural human instinct to prefer to hire people who are similar to you and many appointments are made through personal connections rather than publicly advertised.

An update on another corporate governance review, the Davies Report of 2011, which recommended a target of 25% of FTSE (Financial Times Stock Exchange) listed companies, was issued in 2015. Good progress has been made on having more women non-executive, external directors, but the percentage of executive directors who are women is still very low (4.6% for the FTSE 250).

In addition to the "Old Boys' Network", boards want to appoint people with a strong track record in a particular industry or who have financial expertise. Women tend to have more varied, generalist careers or are professionals in areas such as HR or marketing. There is still a lack of women rising up through the ranks in traditionally male industries such as IT, banking or engineering.

Of course, the whole point of having more diverse boards, with different expertise and backgrounds, is to encourage debate in board meetings and more transparency of information, which is supposed to lead to better governance, innovation and management of risk. Having to explain issues to people who are not expert in your company or industry can help uncover unthinking assumptions and bring fresh perspectives.

Japanese companies in the UK banking and insurance sectors have come under heavy scrutiny from the UK Prudential Regulation Authority. The PRA has the right to interview and approve the appointment of directors to financial sector companies, and also to see the "board pack" (documents for the board meetings) and minutes of the meetings.

Newly appointed Japanese directors have found it very difficult to answer the standard PRA question "why did you choose to take up this role?" when in fact they were simply told to become a director by Japan headquarters. Most board meetings in the UK just rubber-stamped decisions made through *nemawashi* (consensus building) outside the meeting, so the board pack and the minutes were minimal, and in Japanese.

As board diversity increases in Japan, hopefully Japanese companies will become more used to providing a greater quantity of information and more transparency about decision making, which will help the boards of their overseas subsidiaries function better too.

13. JAPANESE BOARDS IN EUROPE SHOULD REFLECT THEIR CUSTOMERS, EMPLOYEES AND COMMUNITY

When I completed the first phase of research into how diverse the European subsidiary boards of the biggest Japanese companies in Europe are, both in terms of the nationality mix of Japanese and European directors, and also the number of women on the board – I was surprised to discover that more boards in Japan had women on them than in Europe. This was surprising if you were expecting boards to reflect the employee mix – particularly the pipeline of managers coming through the ranks of an organisation – as there are without doubt more women employees and proportionally more women managers in Japanese companies in Europe than there are in Japan.

The proportion of directors with European nationalities on the board of Japanese subsidiaries varied wildly from none in the case of Toshiba, Sharp and Fast Retailing (the Uniqlo subsidiary in the UK), through to 100% in the case of Asahi Glass, Bridgestone, Canon and Nidec. So national diversity does not seem to be influenced by which industry the company is in. This also means that what to me is the most compelling case for a diverse board, that it should reflect the customers it is serving, is not the key factor I thought it would be.

20 years' ago, becoming less reliant on Japanese customers abroad as well as in Japan, was the driving force for many Japanese companies embarking on "*kokusaika*" ("internationalization"). Canon was a pioneer

then in appointing Europeans to senior positions in overseas subsidiaries and does, perhaps as a consequence, appear to have fared better than other companies in the consumer electronics sector, both in Japan and in Europe.

The current favoured path to globalization for Japanese companies is through M&A rather than growing international businesses and executives internally, and the major acquisitions of the past decades account for the diverse boards of Asahi Glass (who acquired Glaverbel) and other companies that still have a high proportion of European directors such as Fujitsu (International Computers Ltd), Nomura (Lehman Brothers) and NSG (Pilkington).

There is some sectoral influence. For example, the financial services industry is under intense scrutiny by European regulators who have the power to approve board appointments. They expect directors to have deep understanding and experience of local markets – something which not many Japanese executives can claim.

Both Fujitsu and Hitachi have substantial public sector-oriented businesses in the UK (government services, nuclear power and rail) which means that they not only need to meet the diversity requirements of government purchasing but also gain acceptance of the communities in which they operate. For example, when the board of a Japan-owned UK utility advertised for a director, there was a requirement that applicants be a customer of that utility.

For smaller Japanese companies, or those which are just starting in Europe, it is tempting to stick with a small board with just a couple of non-resident Japanese directors, but as boards come under pressure to have greater transparency and better governance in Europe, appointing local directors from the start should lead to better relations with regulators, customers and employees.

14. INCLUSIVE WORDS

In discussing with a client the way accepted terminology keeps changing in the UK business world, I discovered that "flexible working" is now being renamed "agile working". "Agile" working is meant to have a wider definition than flexible working – the idea being that the focus should be on performance and outcomes, allowing maximum flexibility on the who, what, when and where of executing the work. "Flexible" usually (as it does in Japan) means flexibility on the hours worked and tends to be used when workplaces are trying to be family friendly towards women. "Agile" working implies it is a way of working for every employee.

The client's own job title was another indicator of change – "head of diversity and inclusion". Diversity has become a more commonly used word in Japan now, mainly to mean gender diversity, but increasingly companies are looking at other kinds of diversity such as nationality or sexuality. The reason that "inclusion" has been added to "diversity" in the UK is to ensure that companies don't just focus on targets for diversity, but also how the corporate culture should change to ensure that people with different backgrounds to the mainstream do not feel excluded from decision making or promotion or the everyday conversations and meetings that are going on around them.

Sometimes I find myself thinking that all this emphasis on terminology is irritating and a distraction, but then I remember what it felt like to be a foreign employee in a Japanese company headquarters. I have no complaints about the way I was personally treated, but I regularly used to point out, when asked for my input into English language documents like the annual report – that it seemed alienating to people outside of Japan if employees were broken down into male/female, or Japan-employed and overseas-employed. I knew why these categories existed – because at the time, 99.9% of females were in administrative track jobs, and 100% of men were in management track jobs – so this was a simple way of indicating the ratio of administrative versus line management/sales in the workforce. The Japan-employed and overseas employment figures aligned with the *tantai* (unitary - Japan entity only) and *renketsu* (consolidated) accounting methods.

But it nonetheless made me feel like being female or "overseas" was a lower status. This has all changed now of course, as the distinction between administrative and management track *seishain* (permanent lifetime employees) has disappeared in many companies. With holding companies now being allowed, and changes in accounting methods, the *tantai* and *renketsu* distinction for employees is also less meaningful than it used to be.

I still have Japanese clients consulting me about what to call their various categories of employees however. Some choose "rotating staff" to describe Japanese expatriates – but again this implies that anyone hired outside Japan has no chance of being posted elsewhere. One British employee complained to me about an email from Japan HQ which used the term "subordinate". Even in British class ridden society, we prefer to call all employees "colleagues" or "team members".

15. PROFESSIONAL ACCOUNTABILITY

When the topic of meaningless meetings in Japanese companies comes up in my training workshops, I often tell the story of how I once had to attend a meeting in the Japanese headquarters of the company I was working for, as the representative of the corporate planning department, on a topic I knew nothing about. I was told to read the *ringisho* (circular memo) and not say anything, except for "*ryōkai*" (agreed) at the end. "It was two hours of my life I will never get back. The two people in charge of setting up a loss-making factory simply read out the *ringisho*, line by line and then asked for approval to write off several hundred million yen. This had been approved already, so obviously we just said yes. I still don't know to this day what the meeting was for – perhaps it was a kind of punishment".

On reflection, I think it was about ensuring internal accountability – to give an account of decisions made, actions taken and the reasons behind them. Most Japanese companies have these kinds of mechanisms for internal accountability and their executives are also expected to be accountable to Japanese society for any failures, hence the succession of *shazai* (formal apology) rituals we have seen in recent years.

There is a missing piece though, both in the recent Japanese corporate scandals and also the sexual harassment revelations in the Western media and entertainment industry, which is professional accountability. As Japanese companies globalize and diversify their workforce, I believe they will have to add this piece to their corporate governance and compliance systems.

A wide range of professions in the West, from traditional professions such as law, medicine and accountancy through to newer professions such as HR, investment banking or engineering all have associations to which professionals are expected to belong if they want to practice. They sign up to a set of ethics and regulations and are expected to take exams in order to progress through a series of grades and also undertake a certain number of hours of professional development every year.

Although it has proven tricky to get mutual recognition across countries of professional qualifications, it does help companies build a diverse workforce because they can be "blind" to the gender, age, disability or ethnicity of the person they are hiring, if they have the necessary professional qualifications.

Japanese companies will find it easier to ensure accountability internally and externally when they operate overseas if they employ professionals. Employees who have professional accountability know they will lose their professional status if they do not abide by ethical and regulatory standards, and this gives them the strength to resist any unethical pressure that is put on them by their bosses or customers.

Ensuring accountability is a two-way process, however. Although employees will be accountable internally and to their professional association, their bosses will still be accountable internally and externally for their subordinates' behaviour. This means that bosses must enable an environment of trust, achievable targets and adequate resources.

CHAPTER 4
MANAGING AND COMMUNICATING WITH EUROPEAN COLLEAGUES

1. THE IMPORTANCE OF DEBATE IN EUROPE

A French manager complained to me that when he attends meetings of the European management team (mostly Japanese expatriates based in the Netherlands, where the European headquarters is), he finds out that the decisions have already been made, without his input.

This is a comment I have received frequently over the past 15 years of working with Japanese companies in Europe. I hoped the situation would have improved, as Japanese affiliates localise, and more Europeans are in senior positions, but what seems to have happened is that the communication gap between the senior Europeans and the remaining Japanese expatriates has actually widened, and the senior Europeans feel very cut off from any decision making that happens in Japan headquarters.

I recommend to the European managers a three-step plan to improve relations and communications: 1. People, 2. Process and 3. Particulars. For 'People', they need to build relationships with Japanese colleagues, in Europe and in Japan headquarters. There are obstacles to this – travel expense and rapid rotation of Japanese expatriates. But mutual trust is necessary if Europeans are to be including in the *nemawashi* process.

By 'Process', I mean the *nemawashi* (consensus-based decision making) process needs to be made more explicit and transparent and the purpose of meetings (information exchange or discussion or decisions) needs to be clarified. And for 'Particulars', the European managers need understand the kind of detail and data needed to reassure risk averse executives in Japan.

But this is only half the picture. The Japanese expatriates must accept that their job is not simply to report back to Japan headquarters what is happening in the European subsidiaries. They need to communicate the Japan headquarters' corporate culture, decisions and strategy, and find ways to get European staff feel involved and have a sense of belonging to the wider company.

For Japanese expatriate staff I recommend 1. Debate, 2. Distil and 3. Disseminate. Europeans love to debate – it makes them feel valued, and it is an opportunity to convince them of the direction the company must take, by explaining the background and logic to what is coming out of Japan.

'Distil' means to be clear, precise and concise about what the strategy, corporate culture or decision is. It must be "actionable" – so it can be the touchstone for deciding how to act in a business situation.

'Disseminate' means to take practical steps to make sure that the strategy, corporate culture or decision is communicated to all parts of the European network. This may need to be through cascading information through the correct chains of command if the company is a traditional hierarchical European organisation. Or it could be through workshops, to enable people to have a sense of ownership, and understand how the strategy or corporate culture applies to their daily work. Or it could be through more meetings – but hopefully this time, if 'debate' and 'distillation' have already happened, the meeting attendees will feel more involved and accepting of the outcomes.

2. WHAT JAPANESE COMPANIES CAN LEARN FROM HSBC'S COMPLIANCE STRUGGLES

Descriptions of the difficulties faced by the UK multinational bank HSBC in 2015 reminded me strongly of the challenges faced by Japanese companies which are trying to globalise through acquisition. 2015 should have been the year in which HSBC celebrated 150 years since being founded in Hong Kong by British and Anglo-Indian merchants as a trade finance bank. Unfortunately, this has been marred by a tax evasion scandal at its Swiss private banking arm.

HSBC acquired a Swiss private bank in 1999, a few years after it acquired Midland Bank, one of the UK's "Big Four" retail banks. Then in 2003 it acquired Household Finance, a US consumer finance operation. Up until this diversification of the business, HSBC managed its network of operations through a tight knit group of expatriates (all male until 1989) who were generalists, who had been trained like army officers in a Hong Kong "mess" (similar to a Japanese company dormitories), and were therefore trusted enough to be sent around the world to be the "man on the spot".

This group of generalist managers found it difficult to control businesses that they knew nothing about, in countries they were not familiar with, so local executives from the acquired company were allowed to continue controlling those businesses. The scandal at the Swiss private banking arm was not the only failure of this approach. In 2012, HSBC had to pay a US$1.9bn fine to US authorities for failing to stop the laundering of drug money through its Mexican operation – the banking and financial services company Bital that it acquired in 2002.

If leaving control to local managers is too risky, should Japanese companies who are acquiring overseas subsidiaries continue to try to exert control through Japanese expatriates? This is neither practical, nor the solution. There seems to be a shortage of suitably experienced Japanese managers who can be sent overseas. And like the HSBC expatriates, they are generalists, and will therefore find it hard to understand what is going on in specialist areas of the business in a foreign country.

Without the Japanese expatriate acting as a liaison, conduit and interpreter however, the foreign executives soon find themselves swamped by endless requests for information from the Japan headquarters, supposedly for compliance and risk management purposes. They try to respond to as best they can, but get nothing back in return. It can lead to a sense of not being trusted, and confusion as to the right direction to take.

For HSBC, the solution proposed by many commentators and the CEO himself was to do with having a strong corporate culture and values, and processes for communicating them globally, along with rigorously implemented compliance policies. If this is in place, then a certain degree of autonomy can be given to local managers.

For Japanese companies, where human relationships are so important, to 'process' and 'values' I would add 'people'. In future articles I will look in more detail at these three elements and suggest some practical steps to take.

3. COORDINATION BETWEEN JAPAN HQ AND EUROPEAN SUBSIDIARIES

As I concluded above, Japanese headquarters looking to coordinate effectively with their European subsidiaries needed to consider "people" in addition to having clear communication processes and ensuring there are shared vision and values about how the company should behave.

In the past, many multinationals, not only Japanese companies, relied on a network of expatriate staff to disseminate corporate culture and keep the headquarters informed about what was happening abroad.

Now, Japanese companies are finding that they do not have enough 'global *jinzai*' (globally experienced personnel) at senior levels who are capable of managing their overseas operations, so are having to rely on locally hired senior executives.

These locally hired senior executives often become very frustrated if the communication processes are not clear, and the values and vision are not shared. They find themselves answering the same questions over and over again from multiple divisions in Japan and begin to feel they are not trusted. They are unable to make decisions or propose change and yet do not know who in Japan to ask for support or how to ask them.

This problem does not occur so frequently in Western multinationals because the compliance, authorisation and reporting processes are usually made very clear from the moment a company is acquired or set up. Also, the organisation of people tends to be similar across most Western companies. It's therefore easy for a manager in an overseas subsidiary to work out who their counterpart is, or who the key decision maker might be.

In the European marketing department of one of the Japanese companies I worked for, we had a proposal that needed us to identify and build relationships with many different people in Japan to gain support. In a Western company this would have been easy – there would have been a marketing department, headed by a senior executive (probably EVP level) in the headquarters who would have responsibility for the strategy, vision and brand of the company.

However, in this Japanese company there was no recognisable marketing department. The corporate brand office was more like the compliance part of the PR department – checking that the logo was used correctly. The advertising department simply did whatever each business unit told it to. There was a corporate strategy department, but it did not seem to have any relation to the kind of marketing strategy that Europeans are used to.

I hesitate to say that my conclusion is that Japanese companies have to reorganise their headquarters along Western lines in order to succeed globally, but I do recommend that plenty of attention is given to finding counterparts and making it explicit what the *tantōsha* (person in charge of the daily work) and *madoguchi* (window into an organisation, single point of contact) concepts mean, and identifying who those people should be in the headquarters. This should help reduce the burden of requests going to the local managers and help them build trusting relationships with key people in Japan. Once that is done, attention can be paid to shared values and communication processes.

4. JAPAN HQ IS A BLACK HOLE

One of the German consultants on our team in Europe is a Toyota Production System expert. I asked her what she recommends to mixed Japanese and European teams in the companies she advises, if they are not communicating well. To my surprise, instead of talking about concepts and processes such as *gembashugi* (going to the place where the work is happening) or visualisation, she replied that first of all she gets them to agree on a vision for the team.

I recommended earlier that in order for Japan headquarters to coordinate effectively with their European subsidiaries, they need first of all to look at the people concerned, and make sure there are clearly understood counterparts, *madoguchi* (window into an organisation) and *tantōsha* (person in charge).

It may seem that the obvious next step is to set up communication processes between these people, but I think my German colleague is right, that without a vision for the end goal of this communication, many of these processes will become ineffective or die out.

For example, a British company I advise, who have a subsidiary in Japan, told me that they hold regular global teleconferences for certain business and research areas. However, they discovered that the representative from one of the teams in Japan merely attends the teleconference and does not share what was learned with the rest of their team members. Clearly the Japanese representative does not see the value in cascading further what they heard.

Similarly, the Japanese expatriates at a Japanese manufacturer in the UK told me they all send weekly *hōkoku* (1 pager reports) back to Japan (in Japanese of course), but when in the past they tried to get the British managers involved, the British soon lost interest, seeing it as an additional bureaucratic burden. "It's a black hole", one of the British managers told me. "We send information to Japan but never get anything back". Again, they could not see the benefit to being involved in the communication process. In both this case and the previous case, employees need to feel they are getting information back in return for their input, which is relevant to their jobs.

Many Japanese companies say they have a vision, but in my experience, these are often too vague to be actionable. By actionable, I mean that the vision has enough substance that you can make decisions based on it. Most visions for Japanese B2B manufacturers can be summarised as "contributing to society through innovation" which is actionable to some extent, but means that the company cannot really differentiate itself from its competitors who are saying the same thing. So customers also cannot see the benefit of choosing one supplier over another.

The vision that the company, and the teams within the company have should be differentiated from its competitors, and be actionable. The benefit to behaving in accordance with the vision has to be clear and understood by employees. Once that is in place, the processes for communication and compliance between the headquarters and its subsidiaries will almost take care of themselves.

5. THE EUROPEAN LOVE OF ARGUMENT

I was looking at my diaries from when I was 11 years' old and living in Japan, and was amused to see that I had written in them that my burning ambition was to be a politician. Quite a few of the people I knew at university have become politicians, so I suppose on reflection this was not an impossible dream for me.

I then wondered why I did not try to realise this ambition. I think it is because I really don't like confrontation and I take it too personally. This might be rooted in my childhood in Japan – Japanese schools do not offer as many opportunities to debate as they do in the UK. But I also spent my teenage years in British schools, where, like many schools in the UK and Europe, there were plenty of opportunities to become good at arguing, such as school debating societies and public speaking competitions.

By the time I reached university, I preferred to watch rather than participate in debates. I still enjoyed writing logical, reasoned essays, which are the core of a liberal arts education in Europe, but I did not want to become a journalist either.

Journalism and politics in the UK are very "adversarial" – always insisting that there are two opposed sides to every story and trying to set up a confrontation or show who is to blame. Journalists claim this is a necessary approach, to get to the truth.

However, a common way that politicians and journalists try to dominate the other is by using what are known as "ad hominem" attacks – a Latin phrase which is used in English, meaning "to the man". In other words, they try to undermine the validity of the other person's argument by attacking the personal characteristics of the opponent.

This is not considered a good debating technique, as it is not actually addressing the facts or logic behind the viewpoint or idea being expressed. People try to avoid this kind of technique in the workplace, as it would be seen as discriminatory. Plenty of arguments do take place however, about the definitions, logic, theories, profitability and justifications behind taking various business decisions.

This does not seem to work well with traditional Japanese approach, which is more Confucian and "ascriptive". It's not seen as unfair to assume that someone is more likely to be right because they have a higher status. To the European question of "why?" a Japanese person senses a personal attack and a questioning of authority.

Surprisingly, the nation which is most famous for philosophical rhetoric – France – has an education system which, like Japan, discourages questioning of teachers and therefore of superiors in the workplace. But then France is also famous for its strikes and bloody revolutions. Perhaps this is why in many Northern European workplaces, debate is considered to be "healthy". Japanese managers in Europe need to be prepared to argue their case logically to ensure good employee relations.

6. CALENDARS

Sorting through the various calendars on sale or that were sent to me for promotional purposes I have ended up choosing the same ones as last year – a *haiku* and *ukiyoe* (poetry and art) wall calendar because I like to be reminded of the passing seasons, and a desk calendar that has Japanese and European public holidays on it, for practical reasons.

This annual ritual of picking a calendar reminds me of when I was working at Mitsubishi Corporation in London. We locally hired staff used to fight to grab the desk calendars from Japan left over from mail outs to customers. They not only had photos of the beautiful artefacts from the Seikadō Museum, but could be easily customised so that three months could be viewed at a time, vital for calculating shipping schedules between Japan and Europe.

The publisher of the desk calendar that I chose also shows three months on one page, but I am thinking of suggesting that they further modify their calendar to make it useful to employees of Japanese companies in Europe, by including indicators of the key dates of the Japanese financial year.

Over three quarters of the biggest Japanese companies in Europe run on an April 1st to March 31st financial year in their Japan headquarters. The dates for reporting results and shareholders' meetings in Japan are highly predictable and tend to be clustered by industry. But the annual cycle of proposals and decision making that this sets up, and the midterm plan 3-year cycle that many Japanese companies also adhere to, are not widely understood in Europe.

The majority of European companies run on a calendar year of January to December. But even when the calendar year is used, the dates of when the results are announced or the Annual General Meeting is held vary from company to company by weeks and even months.

European employees therefore need to be actively reminded of key meetings and decision deadlines in Japan headquarters as they do not instinctively know the rhythm of the April to March financial year and it often does not match the rhythms of the British business year. In fact, one British retailing company acquired a few years' ago by a Japanese company found it very hard to comply with the Japanese HQ's request that they submit all their accounts by December 31st, so that the Japan HQ could compile the consolidated accounts in time for their March 31st year end, because this coincided with the UK's busiest time of year - the Christmas shopping period.

The Japan HQ have in fact changed their financial year to January to December a couple of years' ago, giving the need to be more global as the reason. However, when I went back to their British subsidiary last week, and asked them if that helped relieve the pressure, they said they had not really noticed, as the increasingly global nature of their business means they were busy all year round!

7. POINTING AT THE MOON

In January 2013 there was a greater sense of urgency in Japanese companies than in previous quarters, not only to make the numbers, but also to find tangible proof that the strategies in place are the right ones, or if they are not, to draft some radical proposals for the President to make at the end of April, when the year's results must be declared.

It's a predictable part of the annual cycle, but I sense that in recent years, the feeling of crisis is stronger than ever. So many Japanese companies understand that their very existence on the global stage is under question and the cheaper yen will only provide temporary respite from this.

The usual bottom up accumulation of midterm plans, based on projections of the previous years' sales, a chat with customers and "putting a finger in the air", all jammed into several A3 sized sheets of paper, won't do this time.

Some companies will announce, or already have announced, radical restructuring plans, but behind such plans is still the huge question of why the company exists at all – a question that most Japanese companies take very seriously, as so many believe that contributing to society, not just by keeping people in employment, but by making a positive impact on the future shape of the world, is at the core of their being.

This means they have to venture into the touchy-feely territory of vision, values and corporate culture. Something which I believe they are pretty good at communicating to customers and employees in Japanese, but not outside Japan.

Words and numbers are not enough – there need to be stories, heroes and artefacts. Japanese companies have plenty of these, the question is how to communicate them globally.

One example is Alpine Electronics, the Japanese car audio manufacturer. The current chairman, Seizo Ishiguro, talks of how when he headed up the US operation, a cassette deck was returned to the company riddled with bullet holes by an unhappy American customer. The cassette deck is now in Alpine's museum, as a reminder of how the key to Alpine's survival in global markets is the highest possible quality and customer satisfaction.

This is a very tangible artefact, and a great story. Somewhat gentler is the brush painting bought by Sazō Idemitsu, the founder of the Idemitsu petroleum company, when he was 19, at an auction, of Hotei (often known as the Laughing Buddha) pointing to the moon. Apparently he often told employees to "look at the moon" (the big picture) not at Hotei's finger (the details). In other words that Idemitsu was in the petroleum industry not just to make money, but to benefit society.

Intriguingly, in the painting Idemitsu bought, the moon is not depicted at all. It's as if the artist is telling us to go and look for the moon for ourselves. The challenge Japanese companies face is ensuring that this kind of subtlety does not get lost in translation.

8. THE UNQUENCHABLE THIRST FOR INFORMATION

As a homestay student with a Japanese family, I became used to being asked by my host mother where I was going every time I left the house. If it had been my own family, I would probably have responded "Out!" before leaving as quickly as I could, slamming the door behind me. I was trying to avoid my parents interfering in my plans but I soon realised my Japanese home stay mother didn't really have a hidden agenda behind her inquiries – she was simply curious, and wanted to show she cared.

In the Japanese corporate world, there are hidden agendas, but the same thirst for "information for information's sake", continues. A constant niggle I hear from people who aren't Japanese who work in Japanese companies is the sheer quantity of questions, often on seemingly irrelevant details, that they have to deal with from their Japanese colleagues.

These non-Japanese staff worry because they fear that their answers might be seen as commitments and they want to sort out the business case or the strategy before they give the full details of a plan. Or, like my teenage self, they are just concerned that there is some kind of ulterior motive.

I sense that Japanese colleagues are frustrated by this – they want to know the details as soon as possible because they need to feed them back into their network in Japan. If they have "overseas" or "global" in their title then they are supposed to be the instant expert on what overseas operations are doing, regardless of how complex the local cultures and markets are. Their knowledge is currency, or "*neta*" as it is known in Japanese – the inside scoop on how things really are. Japanese people are so used to the idea that in Japanese society nothing is as it really seems, they assume that those who claim to know the real story are the ones with the power and intelligence.

By contrast, many Westerners are surprisingly incurious about the world beyond their immediate sphere. Multinationals run on US lines tend to function on explicit knowledge – distributed through regular updates amongst a select group of global managers, maybe via a weekly phone conference, where predetermined targets are matched against actual figures, and arguments are had about any shortfalls. As a result, US type multinationals send far less headquarters staff out to work in overseas operations than Japanese multinationals, which feel that they need to have a mole in every operation to keep HQ in the loop.

I have some sympathy with the worries of non-Japanese staff. Information casually shared with Japanese colleagues does have a habit of escalating up the Japanese hierarchy and turning into formalised fact, to be thrown back in the face of the overseas staff when commitments never given are not met. Also, Japanese headquarters staff, who are so used to sharing knowledge in informal ways, fail to share it more explicitly with their overseas colleagues.

Information flows need to be two-way to work. Maybe I should have responded to my home stay mother by asking her what she was doing during the day. She might have been pleased to know I cared.

9. THE LACK OF INFORMATION FROM JAPAN - "IT'S LIKE GOLD DUST"

I came back from a trip to Japan clutching various documents from some contacts I met at one particular Japanese company. I asked in advance, before spending too much time translating, if the content was already familiar to the people outside Japan. Apparently it was not and the content was described as "gold dust" by one person.

It's a perennial complaint in the overseas operations of Japanese companies that they don't get enough information from Japan, to the point where they begin to wonder if things are being deliberately hidden from them.

I described in the previous article about the unquenchable thirst for information amongst Japanese employees. In Japan this thirst is partly met through implicit knowledge sharing, by having an open plan office full of people who spend years working together and who all speak Japanese, so do not need to be formal and explicit in the way they communicate. There are more formal communication methods in most departments, such as weekly and monthly reports as well as the infamous A3 sized planning documents and the "*ringi*" proposals, which are circulated around numerous people.

But the problem is these are all in Japanese, and no one feels like taking on the onerous task of translating them into English. They all mostly have higher priority day jobs to attend to. Outsourcing them to a translation agency is one option, but it often takes an insider to truly distinguish what is important and what is really meant by internal documents.

I have come to the conclusion that there needs to be a conscious process set up for communicating between Japanese operations and the rest of the world, and it needs to be a recognised part of someone's job. The person selected for this should not be shunted into some "global" group but be part of the actual business department, otherwise they will not understand the context of the information and which bits are most needed by overseas subsidiaries.

The final piece of the process is identifying the organisational units and people that are counterparts to each other, and therefore need to share information. This is more complicated than it might seem, as most large Japanese companies in my experience are organised in quite different ways to Western equivalents. In Japan there are no sales directors in charge of specific regions or customer segments. There are no marketing directors, in fact there is rarely a standalone marketing department. The organisation is highly vertical, so each business group has to be combed for people who have a global remit or functional role that looks relevant.

This is not easy when few people have written job descriptions. But once the right person and team are found, I am sure their thirst for information from outside Japan and satisfaction derived from being useful to global colleagues will mean the process becomes well embedded.

10. THE VITAL TOOL OF INTERNAL COMMUNICATIONS

It seemed after the 2008 Lehman Shock that the only opportunity for new business for those of us who supply services to Japanese companies, was the continuing wave of Japanese acquisitions. Faced with a saturated, aging market at home and good companies going cheaply overseas, Japanese companies see acquisitions abroad as a way to revitalize and grow.

Western companies were in the mood to accept new Asian owners, too. Weary of the destruction brought about by Anglo-Saxon capitalism, there is plenty of debate going on in Western business circles as to whether it might not be time for a more long-term, stakeholder-oriented – rather than short-term, shareholder-oriented – way of running companies.

We have, of course, been here before. Japan's economic success in the 1980s was attributed to Japanese values – lifetime employment, group orientation, taking the long-term view, striving for growth rather than profit and so on. But then in the 1990s those same values were blamed for Japan's economic failure. The debate as to whether an alternative to the current form of capitalism is truly needed – and whether Confucian capitalism is the best alternative – will no doubt continue.

While the discussion rumbles on, Japanese companies that have acquired overseas companies face the question of how or how not to adapt their distinctive corporate values and cultures.

Regardless of what path is chosen, many Japanese companies have failed to use a vital tool – internal communications. Case in point: A participant at a seminar I gave at a British company that had been acquired two months earlier by a Japanese company carne up to me afterwards, on the verge of tears, to say thank you.

Apparently, I was the first person to talk to her team since the acquisition who was able to explain at a deeper level what was going on. The team members felt they had been left in the dark.

Another participant at a different company mentioned to me that the local operation had only found out a vital piece of news about their company through a U.K. trade magazine.

I have lost count of the number of times Europeans working for Japanese companies have complained to me about information being withheld. When I ask them if they had asked Japanese colleagues for this information, it often transpires that they had not, that they expected to be told.

Many Japanese companies do not have internal communications departments. One director of corporate affairs told me that he could find no counterpart at the new owner's Japan headquarters.

There is an assumption that Japanese employees will pick up corporate strategy and culture through time-honoured methods such as *ishin denshin*, or telepathy. While this assumption cannot, of course, be made for employees who do not work in Japan or who do not speak Japanese, there nevertheless seems to be a fear that translating even innocuous internal documents into English will cause vital secrets to be leaked.

Deliberately leaving it up to employees to work out values and strategies for themselves is itself a corporate value. Once I got used to this, I rather liked it, as it means employees are treated as mature adults. Paradoxically, however, if Japanese companies want to preserve this value as they globalize, it has to be explicitly communicated.

11. ASK RATHER THAN TELL

When I was in a bar in London waiting to go to a Christmas party in 2015, an elderly American man on the table next to me suddenly leaned over and said "can I ask you about Brexit"? It turned out he was a semi-retired Wall Street lawyer, who wanted to gather some insights into what British people were thinking, in preparation for a US–UK conference dinner he was about to attend.

I responded that I would be happy to, so long as I could ask him about the USA as I was going to be interviewed later that week about the impact of Trump's election by a Japanese newspaper. We talked animatedly until I had to leave, and agreed that in these uncertain and confusing times, it was important for global business people to keep talking to each other, so we resolved to stay in touch.

He said he approached me because I looked intelligent and sensible. I suspect I looked that way partly because I had let my hair go silver grey in 2016, to embrace rather than deny my 50th birthday. But what my conversation with him taught me was that rather than simply expecting the wisdom of my older years to be apparent in the way I look and what I say, true wisdom is to seek out the thoughts and opinions of others.

Politicians during elections like to say they are "listening" to people, but of course the people who are most heard are the loudest. During the Brexit and US election campaigns, the loudest people were saying some troublingly racist or sexist or paranoid things. Consequently, many people blocked "others" out, only communicating with friends with the same views on social media.

Listening is not enough – you have to actively seek out people you would not normally talk to and ask them what they think and why. It is something I try to do in my seminars – in fact they are much more fun for me if there are participants who want to share their experiences or come up with alternative solutions, rather than me simply imparting my knowledge.

I often explain to Japanese managers in Europe that Europeans always want to know "why" - so managers must be prepared to give the reasons for their requests. I add that Europeans like to be asked for their opinion, to be consulted. It should not just be a yes or no question. As we saw in the UK and Italy, yes or no referendums can cause confusion rather than clarity in their aftermath, because yes or no questions invite straight rejection, with no way to consult people as to why they rejected it and what they would prefer instead.

My New Year's resolution for 2016 was therefore to seek out the opinions of other people, and ask them why they think that way, while holding back my own views.

12. GIVING FEEDBACK IS NOT JUST A LANGUAGE ISSUE

There has been a marked increase in the number of clients asking me to provide training for Japanese expatriate managers in Europe on giving feedback and performance appraisals. I'd like to think this is because our marketing is having an impact – but on talking to the HR departments of our customers, it seems they have become aware of an increasing number of workplace conflicts between Japanese managers and their teams.

European employee dissatisfaction with Japanese managers' feedback style is not a new issue. Complaints usually include that no feedback is given, or only negative or quantitative feedback. I usually explain that giving feedback is not as embedded in Japanese workplace culture as in Europe. Also, Japanese employees are used to working collaboratively as a team rather than having individual performance evaluated. The best employees are deemed to be the ones who look to improve themselves without having to be told.

I remember when I was working in Japan in the 1990s, many Japanese companies started introducing *seika shugi* (performance-based evaluations) but often not very successfully. Evaluating individuals ended up destroying the collaborative, knowledge sharing work environment that is one of the strengths of the Japanese workplace.

The Japan HQ appraisal systems that have developed since the 1990s are much more quantitative than European systems. The manager gives numerical scores not just for performance and achievement of objectives, but also of behaviours, mindsets and competences. In Europe, we usually just give qualitative assessments of the latter, such as "meets expectations" or "exceeds expectations" or "below expectations".

I suppose the Japanese quantitative approach seems more objective, and less personal. Numbers can be analysed across the whole company, and are not subject to interpretation or language barriers.

European managers use qualitative appraisals to stimulate a dialogue about what expectations they have for each individual and then come to an agreement on development opportunities for individual employees in terms of support that they need from the manager, training needs and potential career paths.

The norms of the workplace are rooted in our educational systems. My experience of the Japanese education system is that exams are of factual knowledge and knowing how to do something, often using multiple choice tests. Such exams assume there are clear right and wrong answers.

European education focuses more on critical thinking and understanding the reasons behind something. Exams are essay based, even in science. Scores are partly on getting the facts or the methodology right, but also on the quality of your arguments and the evidence you bring to prove your point.

Consequently, European employees do not unquestioningly accept numerical scores for individual behaviours, mindset and competences. They expect a manager to set clear expectations, give regular feedback and then be able to explain, with evidence, why the employee has met or not met them when challenged. The millennial generation is particularly demanding in this respect. No wonder Japanese managers need training on this – it's not just a language issue.

13. IS VIDEOCONFERENCING THE SOLUTION TO LACK OF COMMUNICATION WITH JAPAN HQ?

I became involved in a large number of video conference calls in 2010–2013 due to my role in a global team, and had to revise my opinion of their effectiveness, in a positive sense, thanks to the technological improvements of recent years. But when it comes to communicating with Japanese counterparts, video conferencing is still no replacement for face-to-face meetings.

The issues involved in remote communication with what are known as "high context" cultures like Japan are well documented. People from such cultures prefer communication that relies on nonverbal cues such as body language, silences and voice tones. People from low context cultures (the US, Germany and Australia, for example) prefer explicit verbal communication.

It would seem, then, that video conferencing is the next best thing to meeting a high-context person face to face, and certainly preferable to e-mail and phone calls. My impression so far is that it can work, but mostly for regular, formal group meetings.

Even then though, there are some problems. Firstly, the native English speakers don't realise that the way they are speaking – conversational, lots of "witty" asides and sentences which tail off – is alienating the group at the other end. All the classic Japanese group meeting behaviours start to emerge – eyes shut, furrowed brows or side conversations to clarify comprehension and intention.

The solution to this is to speak "international" English – clear short sentences, lots of clarifying and comprehension checking statements and questions and use of visible agendas, notes and slideware.

Still, differing expectations about the functions of meetings can affect the outcomes of a video conference. In Japan, decisions are reached outside of formal meetings. A person wanting to make a proposal will talk informally to all possible people affected, and maybe send around a proposal which will be marked as approved by all the different teams concerned. A meeting might then be called, but it will be for rubber stamping purposes, to report back or to draw up action points. In western cultures, however, meetings are seen as the chance to brainstorm or resolve differences.

Finally, there is one vital piece of communication that video conferencing cannot enable – "informal contact." In Japan much of the negotiating and trust building is done outside formal meetings – in pubs, karaoke bars and restaurants. It's the infamous *honne* and *tatemae* problem – there is the official opinion, which will be expressed in group meetings but to know the real story, you have to be out of the office, talking one to one, or amongst a select few.

Face to face continues to be necessary from time to time, not just in the first phase of virtual team building. I've had plenty of beers and trust building with Japanese colleagues over the years, but when speaking one to one on the phone, in Japanese, they sometimes cannot be straight with me. The reason for this is not profound – open plan offices are the norm in Japan, so everyone can hear what you say.

14. THE DIFFERENCE BETWEEN JAPANESE AND DUTCH CONSENSUS BUILDING

Quite a few Europeans working in Japanese companies are aware of *nemawashi*, often described as "Japanese style consensus building". When I talk about *nemawashi* in my training sessions, I translate it as "preparing the ground" or "doing the spadework." I try to create a more vivid image by pointing out that if you want to transplant a mature tree, just yanking the tree out of the ground by the trunk will kill it. The metaphor holds if the goal is to transplant a new idea in a Japanese company. If you were approach whoever you think has the decision-making authority ('the trunk') and obtain only their approval, it is likely the decision would die in implementation, because you did not get the understanding or agreement of all the other people likely to be affected or interested (the roots).

Europeans from consensus oriented national cultures like those of the Netherlands and Sweden, respond to this lesson by saying "well of course, we would always do this kind of consensus building anyway, it's common sense." In the Netherlands, consensus-based decision making is known as the polder model. Polders are low lying tracts of reclaimed land protected from the sea by dykes. In the past, all Dutch, regardless of whether they were peasants or noblemen, whether they lived on or near the polders, had to reach a consensus on how to protect them, and everyone had to be involved in carrying out the plan, otherwise all would suffer. Nowadays the word describes the kind of political consensus reached between government, the unions and business to adjust wages or social benefits or environmental protection.

Both Dutch and Japanese would therefore say they have a long history of consensus-based decision making, but a study published in the Journal of

Management Studies[3] concludes that "the concept of consensus is interpreted quite differently by Japanese and Dutch managers." In Japanese companies, *nemawashi* is carried out through a series of informal, often one-on-one discussions, so that there is already a consensus when the meeting to discuss the "transplantation" is held. The meeting, then, is more about formally recognising the decision. In Dutch companies, the consensus is reached during a meeting, often through quite heated debate. Also, the Japanese managers demand a more complete consensus, whereby all agree, including other departments, whereas Dutch "appreciate the process of trying to reach consensus, but when a difference of opinion persists, the decision is taken by someone".

This someone would therefore be expected to take responsibility for the decision, if things were to go wrong. In Japan, the view is that a comprehensive consensus is necessary to avoid putting the decision maker and the company at risk, and to preserve harmony and the employee loyalty. Given the time and care taken to get such a comprehensive consensus in Japan, once a decision is made, there is no turning back. To the Dutch, this is symptomatic of Japanese companies, where "everyone has responsibility, but nobody can take responsibility".

15. SITUATIONAL LEADERSHIP

One of the issues that Japanese people who come to work in Europe find most challenging is the multiple nationalities of people they have to work with. Whether you are based in London, Duesseldorf or Amsterdam, it is highly likely that your colleagues will be a mixture of not just British, German or Dutch but also Romanian, Lithuanian, Polish, Spanish or indeed Indian or Chinese.

---

[3] Comprehensiveness versus Pragmatism: Consensus at the Japanese-Dutch Interface, *Niels G. Noorderhaven, Jos Benders and Arjan B. Keizer,* Journal of Management Studies, 2007

Much of the global leadership or management training that is offered in Japan is based on American models. Europeans are used to American management styles, so they will tolerate them - at least superficially. However, many of these "one size fits all" models are not ultimately effective in getting Europeans to go beyond superficial compliance. In fact, they can have quite a demotivating effect, particularly if they are too rigidly focused on quantitative targets and objectives.

European managers themselves find that the American model which works the best is known as "situational leadership". This is not a new theory – it was developed in the 1960s and 1970s by the Americans Dr Paul Hersey and Ken Blanchard. It suits the European context because the key idea is that there is no one best style of leadership, and situational leaders are those who are able to diagnose the situation, adjust their leadership style and communicate accordingly. They also need to be able to take account of the "performance readiness" – in other words the ability and willingness – of the various members of the team.

National cultural differences are not specifically mentioned in the model, but in my training I always relate situational leadership to what is known about the preferences in each European country for top down or consensus oriented decision making styles, as well as direct or indirect and formal or informal communication in the ways of giving feedback or direction.

Of course, this can be somewhat overwhelming for someone who is new to the European workplace. It is particularly tough for Japanese people who have worked in the more traditional Japanese companies, where people just do as best they can whatever their bosses tell them, whether they are willing or able or not.

But I think Japanese managers have two big advantages. Although this is a generalization and may not apply to all Japanese managers, in my twenty-five years' experience of working with or in Japanese companies, most of the Japanese people I have met have been humble about their own abilities and also curious about other cultures. This means they are willing to learn and to accept that their usual way of working may have to be adjusted.

16. JAPANESE LEADERS NEED MORE CONFIDENCE IN A JAPANESE STYLE GLOBALIZATION

Many of our Japanese client companies are embarking on global initiatives, in marketing or human resources, and consciously involving overseas employees in them. It's great to see positive, forward thinking even in these difficult times, but comments I have been getting from the Europeans involved in these initiatives have been puzzling me.

Normally, discussions in our European training sessions about decision making in Japanese companies revolve around *nemawashi* (literally, going around the roots of a tree) a consensus based, largely bottom up, decision making system common in Japanese companies. This decision-making process may be an entirely bottom up initiative, or triggered by a vague top down directive.

Consensus based decision making is not uniquely Japanese of course. In Europe, plenty of national and corporate cultures prefer some kind of consensus-based approach, instead of top down imposition. However, when the Europeans involved in the global initiatives have tried to get a consensus-based dialogue going with Japan, they instead been met with passivity from their Japanese counterparts.

One British director told me that he had suggested to his Japanese team that they come up with a proposal for a new workflow. Because they looked puzzled, he scribbled on a whiteboard very roughly what he had in mind. To his concern, the final proposal simply replicated his rough sketch. "When I put ideas to teams in Europe that I have led, I expect them to push back. After all, they often know far better than I do what can or can't be done".

Another British manager proposed a series of discussion sessions with Japanese marketing staff, to give feedback into a new brand strategy, only to be met with a request that the European team "just tell us what to put in the advertising".

This could of course be due to a reluctance to have open confrontation, particularly in English. But I also sense an attitude that because the initiatives are "global" and come dressed in English "marketing" and "strategy" terminology unfamiliar to Japanese people, the Japanese employees feel it is not their area of expertise, so they should just let the "Western" side of the team take the lead.

Yet this is precisely what these European managers are trying to avoid. They want to take an approach to creating strategy which is culturally sensitive. After all, "global" these days does not mean just the West, but China, India and elsewhere. The European managers were rather hoping their Japanese colleagues would have a better cultural understanding of how to incorporate the Asian operations into the initiatives than they did.

How then could the Japanese employees engage in a dialogue in a way that does not make them feel uncomfortable? I would suggest the "coaching" style, which comes naturally to many Japanese people I have worked with. This means that instead of openly stating a disagreement, the listener asks questions which help the presenter to see the problems in their proposal themselves, rather than be told what is wrong.

Overall though, Japanese managers should have more confidence in themselves as leaders of a Japanese style globalization, which may, let us hope, work rather better than Western style globalization has so far.

Pernille Rudlin

CHAPTER 5. UNDERSTANDING EUROPE - BREXIT AND BEYOND

1. SPRING CLEANING

Japanese people living in northern Europe tell me they miss the distinctive four seasons of Japan. At first this seems a strange thing to say to most Europeans, as we believe we have four distinct seasons too. But it is true that changes in the season are far less predictable than in Japan, and from autumn through to spring there can be a succession of indistinguishable grey, wet, cold days.

Spring came earlier than normal in 2016 thanks to an unusually warm winter. The daffodils and crocuses were already beginning to bloom in February in the parks where I walk my dog and my husband and I remarked how busy and energised the town seemed. Although the end of season sales were still dragging on, the new spring stock came in, with fresh, lighter colours in the window. The bright sunshine pushed me outdoors to clean the outside of our windows of the winter grime and my husband finished repainting the kitchen.

We call this "spring cleaning" in the UK – similar to the ōsōji (Big Clean) that happens in Japan for the New Year. We don't do much cleaning around New Year partly because the days are so short – getting dark by 4pm with the sun rising as late as 8am at the end of December. Even in the daylight hours it is too gloomy to see the dirt.

Spring is also a time of rebirth and renewal in the Christian calendar. In 2016 Lent was from February 10th to March 24th, when you were meant to give up vices such as drinking alcohol or smoking or eating favourite foods such as chocolate. This is a way of remembering the 40 days that Jesus spent fasting in the desert and is supposed to be a spiritual preparation for Easter which commemorates the death and resurrection of Jesus. These dates change from year to year – Easter and Lent in 2017 will be three weeks later than 2016.

Actually, the word "Easter" has pre-Christian origins – deriving from an old Germanic word for dawn. According to the 8th century historian,

Bede, there was a northern European pagan goddess of dawn, Eostre, whose symbol was a hare or rabbit – which is thought to be why so many Easter decorations feature rabbits. Another symbol of Easter, the egg, either made from chocolate or painted hen's eggs, is also pre-Christian, when people gave each other eggs as gifts around the time of the spring equinox.

So, while the financial year of April 1st to March 31st is not as universal in Europe as it is in Japan, and our academic year actually starts in September/October, March and April are still a good time to renew and refresh the company. The rhythms of a cleansing and preparation period in February and March, followed by a new lease of life in April have deep roots in the European psyche.

2. MARGARET THATCHER'S LEGACY

I suspect it was hard for people in Japan to understand why Margaret Thatcher's death in 2013 aroused such strong feelings of hatred and adulation amongst British people, even 23 years after she ceased to be prime minister.

My generation (people born in the 1960s) is sometimes labelled "Thatcher's children" – because we grew up under her. We remember 1971, when she was education minister and abolished free school milk for seven to eleven-year-old school children. Actually, many children, myself included, really disliked the free school milk, which was lukewarm and smelly by the time we were given it to drink at morning break each day.

We had already moved to Japan by the time I was seven. I did not escape, however, as we had to drink milk at my Japanese school too, which was even worse tasting, in my opinion, because it was homogenised rather than pasteurised.

People thought we were crazy to move to somewhere as foreign as Japan, but England in 1972 did not feel like a comfortable place to be either – there had been miners' and dockers' strikes, followed by declarations of a state of emergency. Wage and price freezes had been announced and unemployment went over 1 million for the first time since the 1930s.

There were economic problems in Japan too – I remember the toilet paper panic buying because of the oil crisis – but as is now well known, the crisis was the trigger for Japan to start innovating in car manufacturing. Just before we left the UK, Honda had started importing cars to the UK, and when we returned to the UK in 1977, we decided to buy a Datsun Sunny 120Y.

My grandparents were horrified. They still had strong memories of the war and had opposed us moving to Japan. They could not understand why we did not buy a British car, like the Triumph Dolomite they owned. It was manufactured by British Leyland, which was then being crippled by a series of strikes.

Margaret Thatcher was extremely patriotic too – but she was happy to welcome any foreign investor who shared her ethic of hard work. While my generation was busy hating her for destroying mining communities, cutting education spending and warmongering, her government encouraged Nissan to open its first factory, in Sunderland, an area in desperate need of jobs thanks to the closure of mines and shipyards.

Thirty years later, there are no British owned volume car producers, but over 1.5 million vehicles were produced in the UK in 2015, closing in on the 2 million peak of 1970, and 86% of production is exported. Only 195,000 people are directly employed by the car industry, however, compared to 850,000 in 1970. The North of England remains a high unemployment, depressed region. This explains the depth of feelings about Mrs Thatcher's legacy – she was right, from a business perspective, but there was a human cost which was not addressed.

3. ANTI AMERICANISM IN EUROPE

For people of my age, the election of Donald Trump brought back memories of when Ronald Reagan was elected, thirty-five years' previously. I remember, as a teenager, the British pop songs and TV programmes that mocked Americans for electing Reagan – a seemingly dumb, war mongering, B movie actor.

I lived in Pennsylvania for half a year just before Reagan's election, and attended an American high school. It was a formative experience for me, to see for myself the land of opportunity, where everything seemed new, energetic and plentiful, compared to the recession, high unemployment and riots back in the UK.

Most Europeans, not just the British, have these similarly mixed feelings about the US and the American people – of admiration, resentment and fear. My parents and grandparents remember the American GIs who were stationed in Europe – to whom they were both grateful for helping liberate Europe – but also resentful of how much wealthier and better fed they seemed than the rest of the population.

I suspect many Japanese people also share these feelings and memories. However, the American influence on Japan is even stronger, thanks to the long post war occupation, the continuing influence of American popular culture, and the fact that the English taught in Japanese schools is American English.

There is a tendency therefore in Japan for those who do not know other Western cultures, to think that the American communication style will work everywhere. But Europeans are very sensitive to anything that Japanese companies do which seems too obviously American. If Japanese companies try to manage their overseas operations via their US subsidiaries, resentments rapidly build up in Europe about the top-down, highly controlling American management style.

Japanese expatriates who arrive in Europe after experience in the US become frustrated, because the American "just do it" approach to directing subordinates does not work. It is not as easy to fire people for incompetence or unwillingness to follow direction in Europe as it is in the USA. Europeans expect to be consulted about their work and think it is important to raise objections or point out problems to their bosses if there are justifiable concerns.

Even written materials which are too obviously American can cause resistance. Twice now I have been told by clients that they did not want to roll out e-learning and manuals which had been developed in Japan, using American style English and tone.

American companies are good at persuading Japanese customers that the American way is the globally accepted international standard way and that is true to some extent. However, the best solution, which we also use at Japan Intercultural Consulting for our training, is to have American core material - so that our customers get the same basic approach around the world - but allow a great deal of customisation to suit the tastes of specific countries.

Getting this balance right is not easy, but if the effort is not made, stubborn European resistance and rejection will result.

4. OVERCOMING BRITISH NEGATIVITY

According to a poll in 2015, only 7% of UK companies were willing to speak out in favour of the UK staying in the European Union, even though two thirds believed leaving the EU would be damaging for them. Of course, the Greek crisis made it difficult to say anything positive about Europe, but I also think the British have a strong preference for talking negatively rather than positively, when asked to make a commitment to something, particularly if they feel there are plenty of downsides to getting involved.

Then, like the British professor of economics I met in 2015 - who not only forecast the 2008 Lehman shock but also advised the UK against joining the euro - we can say, smugly, "I told you so", when things go wrong. This apparent wisdom does not, however, take into account what might have happened if we British had got involved. Maybe the Eurozone would have been better structured and managed, or a more balanced approach taken to Greece's membership conditions and current difficulties if the UK had participated, not only to point out the problems, but find solutions.

I've noticed when working in European teams that British pragmatism acts as a good counterbalance to French rhetoric and German methodological rigour. Both Japanese and American managers are united however, in finding the British urge to be upfront about all the likely problems and obstacles, without suggesting any solutions, very frustrating.

Americans want to "just do it" and are not interested in the past, whereas the British look to history and their own experience, so as not to repeat mistakes. A Japanese manager who had become used to the American management style said to me "how do I motivate British staff? In the US, my team will do as I ask, because I can promise them a bonus or threaten to fire them if they don't do it, but the British team don't seem to be so motivated by money, and they know it's a lot harder to fire them here than in the US."

Some British employees are of course motivated by money, particularly in the financial sector, but for most British workers the motivation is more around self-fulfilment, a chance to put their expertise and experience into practice, to make a difference. So if they believe that they will not be able to do something, they won't even try, as they know how demotivating and humiliating failure will be.

I discussed with the Japanese manager the concept of *"jinji wo tsukushite, tenmei wo matsu"* (do all that is humanly possible, then wait for the heavens to decide) – that Japanese also have a sense of fatalism, but that does not preclude doing whatever you can to make something work. I described this conversation to a senior British executive, and she started smiling ruefully. It turned out she had insisted to a Japanese boss that a particular course of action was not feasible. He had persuaded her (I expect through appealing to her expertise and experience) and so she eventually went ahead, and to her surprise, she succeeded.

5. THE BALKANS AND EUROPE

On the way to the stunning Krka waterfalls in Croatia, from where we staying on the Adriatic coast for our holidays in 2015, our tour guide suddenly said "we are now in the Balkan part of Croatia". The term Balkan has many resonances for Europeans who know their history. Not only is it 20 years since the war in the Balkan peninsula, but it is 100 years since

WWI, which was thought to partly have been the result of "Balkanization", whereby the countries, formerly ruled by the Ottoman Empire or the Austro-Hungarian empire, fragmented into warring states. Clearly our guide wanted us to appreciate that Croatia was not just Balkan, but also Mediterranean, and therefore part of modern Europe.

The warring Balkan states were in part reunified under the Soviet Union after WWII and most Western Europeans of my generation remember the Adriatic coast as being part of Yugoslavia, and a cheap but pleasant place to go on holiday. Yugoslavia was meant to be one of the more benign and successful Soviet satellite countries, so it was a shock to Western Europeans when it collapsed into a bloody civil war.

Croatia became the most recent member to join the European Union, in 2013. Other Balkan countries such as Former Yugoslav Republic of Macedonia, Serbia and Montenegro are official candidate countries, with Bosnia and Herzegovina being considered a "potential candidate".

With the European Union in danger of falling apart itself, thanks to the Eurozone crisis and the UK referendum on exiting, the Balkan candidate countries must wonder what exactly the benefit of joining the EU might be. For them, the original aim of the European Union, to prevent outbreaks of further wars through economic cooperation, still has meaning, of course, given their recent history.

The benefits of economic cooperation are less obvious. It is clear from Croatia's recent accession that joining the EU later on means missing out on the big regional business investments by multinationals. Balkan state populations and economies are relatively small, so there is not much incentive to invest substantially in opening a subsidiary in such countries – the markets could probably be easily covered through a local agent, or from a regional base in Germany or Poland.

Croatia still has a shipbuilding industry, representing 10% of its exports but clearly it has had to concede that a major economic driver is going to be tourism, as it was in the past. I saw plenty of Japanese tour groups there, and I expect, like us, they were impressed by the beauty and history of Croatia's old towns, the delicious seafood and how clean and well looked after the streets and buildings were.

Above all what really struck me was the hardworking, efficient, polite, honest, well educated, excellent English ability and cheerful nature of all the Croatians we met. Although the Croatian market may not be attractive to foreign investment, the Croatian workforce certainly is.

6. ESTONIA - IN SEARCH OF EUROPE'S COMMON CULTURE

I have been wanting to visit Estonia for a while. Although it is a tiny country, with only 1.3 million population, I knew from the research that had been done on my family history in the Baltic region that Estonia's story would help me understand more about the development of Europe and whether there could be such a thing as a European identity or common culture.

So when I had an opportunity to visit the Estonian capital, Tallinn, for a conference, I made sure I had plenty of time for sightseeing. I know Japanese people often think of Europe as having a "stone culture" – buildings built to last, as opposed to buildings made of wood which can be pulled down as needed, and Estonia certainly fits that category, with plenty of beautiful churches and medieval houses built from the local limestone to visit.

However, there were other aspects of Estonia which did not fit my usual concept of a European country. For example, Christianity came very late to Estonia, in the 13th century, a thousand years after it arrived in Western Europe. It was a pagan country until it was conquered by the Northern Crusades, led by the Christian Kings of Denmark and Sweden and the German Livonian and Teutonic military orders (which is where my mother's family had their roots). To this day Estonia is one of Europe's least religious countries.

The late arrival of Christianity was partly because Estonia was never occupied by the Romans – unlike most other Western and Southern European countries. Estonia was, however, occupied by other countries for the past 700 years; Sweden, then Russia, then a brief moment of independency in the 1920 and 1930s, then Germany and then most recently by Communist Russia, when it was part of the Soviet Union.

The Russians tried to industrialise what was basically an agricultural and trading economy, setting up factories and mines, bringing in many Russians to work in them. Initially Estonia was seen as a prosperous place to emigrate to but the industrialization was not successful, and the Estonian economy suffered, particularly as its usual trade routes to the West had been cut off.

It was when I wandered around the old merchant houses of Tallinn that I felt I was in a recognisably European environment. The merchants of Tallinn were part of the Hanseatic League, a confederation of merchants and towns that stretched across many countries of Northern Europe, from the UK to Russia from the 13th to the 17th centuries.

Even now, with the rise of anti-European movements in the UK and the Netherlands, most people would want to stay in some kind of trade federation. The region's history of trading and shipping, travelling and migrating around Europe and a love of doing deals with each other is still very strong. It's an identity nobody in Europe wants to lose.

7. UK MAY DRIVE AWAY JAPANESE FIRMS IF IT TRIES TO "BE LIKE NORWAY"

Charles Grant, of the Centre for European Reform, spoke to the Japanese Chamber of Commerce and Industry in the UK in 2013 on the likelihood that there would be a referendum in 2016 on whether the UK retains its membership of the European Union or leaves. He predicted that the referendum would result in a vote for the UK to break away.

The reasons he gave were that the British pro-European campaign was not as well funded as the anti-European campaign, and there were plenty of Euro-sceptic politicians of all political persuasions. The British media was also mainly prejudiced against Europe in its coverage.

The arguments for the UK staying in the EU are mostly technical, to do with foreign direct investment and the economic impact, whereas the anti-

European campaign can make an emotional appeal, by invoking threats to national sovereignty.

British business people may be generally in favour of continuing as members, but I agree with Charles Grant that there is a lack of enthusiasm, and a certain complacency about what will happen if the UK does leave. British businesses think the UK can be like Norway - prosperous, part of some kind of free trade area, but independent. In actual fact, Norway is not as immune as it may seem from EU policies, and yet has no influence over setting those policies.

From my Japanese business perspective, "being like Norway" would be disastrous for the UK. I have seen a slow trend towards consolidation across Europe over the past ten years amongst my seventy or so Japanese clients, with the UK playing an important role as the coordinating European headquarters, drawing on a pool of talented Europeans who can easily move to and from the UK thanks to the open borders within the European Union, either working for the headquarters itself or for professional support services such as lawyers, accountants and consultants.

Japanese companies now employ 437,000 people across Europe, according to JETRO, and the UK is by far the biggest beneficiary, with over 140,000 employees of Japanese companies, compared to Germany with 59,000. Germany still has a strong attraction for Japanese multinationals, however, particularly those which are more engineering oriented. If the UK shut its borders and stopped being an influence in the EU, it's not hard to imagine Japanese companies shifting their European headquarter functions over to Germany – or the Netherlands.

All the Japanese business people resident in the UK with whom I have spoken want Britain to stay in the European Union. However, they are afraid to speak out, for fear that this would seem like foreigners trying to interfere in domestic politics. It is going to be up to British businesspeople like me, whose companies are active across the European Union, to make the case. It cannot just be about jobs for the UK, but also Britain's image globally, and how it will be damaged by "Little Englander" isolationism. If we do not seem to want to play our part in globalisation, to be influential and proactive, the global players will take their ball elsewhere.

8. BRITISH PRAGMATISM, SCOTTISH INDEPENDENCE AND BREXIT

[This article was written in September 2014]

The opinion polls during the Scottish independence referendum are very close right up to the vote. It looks as if the "the heart will rule the head" – the rational head saying "no" to independence, but the heart excited by "yes" to becoming a separate nation again, in charge of its own destiny, after 300 years of union with the UK.

Businesses, Scottish and English, have finally started speaking out, mostly for the "No Thanks" side of the campaign, but "no" is not very appealing word and the reasons for "no" can sound like scaremongering. The future is uncertain for an independent Scotland. Not only will difficult negotiations start on whether and how Scotland will be able to keep the sterling pound as its currency, but also negotiations will have to begin with the European Union as to whether and how soon Scotland can become a member nation.

The UK is also less than a year away from a General Election in May 2015, which the Conservative Party is fighting on a promise of a referendum of the UK's membership of the EU. The UK Independence Party, which supports leaving the EU, has done very well in recent local and European elections, so it is a real possibility that if the Conservatives form the next government, the British people will vote to leave the European Union.

It must seem odd to Japanese business people that British citizens would willingly vote for actions which might undermine the political and economic stability that has made the UK such an attractive destination for foreign investment. But it is that very history of stability that seems to give Scottish and other British people the confidence that somehow everything will be all right. We pride ourselves on being pragmatic, and that we will somehow "muddle through". Businesses are making contingency plans for Scottish independence and no doubt for any Brexit (British exit of the EU) too.

Edinburgh, the capital of Scotland, is the second financial city in the UK after London, but even the Royal Bank of Scotland says it is considering moving its headquarters to England if Scotland becomes independent. The other major sector in Scotland, the oil industry, has been unnerved by threats of nationalization should the Nationalists gain power. All sectors are worried that corporate taxes may have to rise to fund the Nationalists' progressive policies or else that Scotland's creditworthiness will be affected.

Unsurprisingly, Japanese companies (and other non-UK companies) have not spoken out on the issue, as this would be counterproductive, but as many Japanese banks, construction and engineering firms have invested in social infrastructure projects in Scotland and the rest of the UK, the hope must be that even if Scottish hearts win the vote for independence, the famously "canny", rational Scottish heads will prevail afterwards and British pragmatism will also avoid too much upheaval in the coming years of renegotiations with the EU.

9. FRANCE

As the UK approached a general election in May 2015, the coalition government was under pressure to explain how it was going to meet its commitment to cut immigration to the UK to tens of thousands. The clampdown on non-EU immigration by the UK government had been causing plenty of concern amongst the Japanese business community for some time. The government can control non-EU immigration, but not the hundreds of thousands of immigrants who come from EU countries to the UK each year, because of the EU commitment to the principle of free movement of labour. This is why Japanese companies are finding it so hard to get visas for their Japanese expatriate staff.

Angela Merkel stated that if the UK tries to undermine this principle of the free movement of labour within Europe, the coalition government could even find themselves having to leave the EU. Pro Europeans and most businesspeople in the UK would rather further reforms were made to the

EU, which address the causes of pan-European movements of people, but this would mean further harmonisation of business and labour regulations. Anti-Europeans are antagonistic towards any imposition of unified regulations and the unions in countries such as France or Germany would resist any reforms which would threaten protection of employment of their members, or reduce state benefits.

For example, it is estimated there are over 300,000 French people living in London, making it the sixth biggest French city in terms of population. The usual explanation for this is that young people have found it hard to get a permanent job or start a business in France. There are more opportunities for them in the UK.

I've certainly found, as I have been expanding my business in France, that the bureaucracy and barriers to efficiency in France are quite bewildering compared to the UK. For example, in order to sell training courses to a French company, I have to hire an agent who is a registered company in France, and also is an approved training provider. This agent then has to provide all kinds of paperwork to the customer, so they can claim back from a state training fund the training taxes they have contributed. This adds considerable expense and delays to my business.

A Japanese company told me that when they tried to acquire a French software company that was about to go bankrupt, the employees decided they would prefer the company go bankrupt even though they would lose their jobs, because then they would have 80% of their salary, benefits and even mortgages paid for the next three years.

I can see that from the French perspective these regulations and taxes can be justified as ways of creating and retaining jobs and ensuring development of skills, but in reality all it has done is deter foreign companies from making any significant investments in France. So despite the visa difficulties, the UK is still the destination of choice in Europe, for businesses and people.

10. WHY THE REFUGEE CRISIS MIGHT MEAN THE END OF THE EU

When I asserted that Britain leaving the EU would result in many multinationals withdrawing their European headquarters from the UK, a British person of Greek origin claimed that the UK would be fine on its own. It would be better off without burdensome EU regulations enforced by a cabal, he said, and the UK is such an innovative country, companies would want to base themselves here whatever our European status.

Given the treatment of Greece by the European institutions recently, I suppose this view is not surprising. There have been many complaints in the UK too about too much European regulation. Often though, as in the case of an EU standard on the amount of noise a lawnmower can emit, these regulations were actually promoted by British officials because they benefited British manufacturers. For manufacturers in general, the comfort in setting up a factory anywhere in the EU is that by meeting these standards, their products will be approved to sell anywhere in the 28 countries of the EU.

If the UK were to leave the EU, it would no longer be able to influence these regulations, and yet would have to abide by them if it wanted to sell its products in its closest and biggest market. Fortunately, for British people like me who are pro-European, the new leader of the opposition Labour Party has just said that he would campaign to stay in the European Union in the forthcoming referendum (likely next year).

There had been some doubt about this, because it is assumed that the Prime Minister David Cameron, in his negotiations with the EU member states, is trying to weaken the social charter of the European Union, which has brought about protection for employees in terms of working time, holidays, discrimination, etc. The Labour Party, as you can tell by the name, is strongly committed to supporting the rights of working people, so has decided to campaign for staying in the European Union, regardless of the deal Cameron reaches, by committing to reverse any social concessions gained, should Labour get back into power.

One of the key non-negotiables for the core European states such as France or Germany - which actually is one of the main reasons many British citizens oppose the European Union - is the free movement of people. To me, this is why the UK is as innovative as it is. There is plenty of evidence that diversity encourages innovation and London is without doubt one of the most diverse cities in Europe. If you locate your company in the London area, you can access an extraordinary range of nationalities, viewpoints and skills, all with English as the common language.

The current refugee crisis is weakening this commitment to the free movement of people and could even bring about the end of the European Union entirely. Instead of coming up with a coordinated solution, member countries are behaving like they have not remembered the lessons of the two World Wars we are currently commemorating.

11. WHAT JAPANESE COMPANIES SHOULD DO, IF THE UK LEAVES THE EUROPEAN UNION

When I moved to Norwich in 2014, my new bookkeeper unnerved me by saying "we don't do euros round here". A third of my turnover is in euros, so I wondered whether I had chosen the best location for my business. It's true that there aren't that many Japanese companies – my target customer group - locally either. However, those that are in the region reflect the east of England's strengths in food processing and wind energy.

It is also easy to access the City of London from Norwich. It was one such City based company - recently acquired by a Japanese insurance company - that took me to Belgium in 2015.

I decided to take the opportunity to visit Bruges, intrigued by its similarities to Norwich. Both were thriving river ports in the medieval period, trading in locally made cloth. Both missed out on the industrial revolution and trade declined after their respective rivers silted up. But whereas tourism is now the main economic driver for Bruges, Norwich has diversified, into insurance and other professional services.

Bruges is where Mrs Thatcher made her famous 1988 speech against further European integration. The Bruges Group, many of whose members are behind the current campaign for Britain to leave the EU, took their name from this speech.

These campaigners see exiting the European Union as a means of ending European political and regulatory interference. However, for ordinary British people, the argument that most resonates is that of getting back control of the UK's borders, and preventing further immigration, particularly from Europe.

Other ports on the UK's east coast have not fared as well as Norwich. Unemployment is high yet large numbers of Europeans have come to the region to help with the harvesting and production of food. UKIP, the party which wants Britain to leave the European Union, has significant local support. They promote the view that European immigrants are taking British jobs, keeping wages low, and putting pressure on schools and the health service.

So what should Japanese companies do if the UK does leave the EU? Presumably those that have already invested – either because the UK had a strength in a particular industry, or they wanted to access the UK market – will stay. But those who use the UK as a coordination base for the rest of Europe, may well consider relocating or shifting any further investment into continental Europe.

The common market and free movement of people over the past 40 years in Europe has brought about a more integrated structure for most multinationals. The UK has benefited from this by becoming the main host of European headquarter functions, generating direct and indirect employment. This has made London an expensive place to operate, so jobs are already moving east, not just to the east of the UK, but to countries like Poland. I am also now looking to recruit a consultant in Poland. Ironically, most of the candidates have had experience working in the UK.

12. THE FORTH BRIDGE BREXIT

The British have a saying for when a job is never finished – "painting the Forth Bridge". The Forth Bridge is a nineteenth century railway bridge, nearly 2.5km long, near Edinburgh. It has a very distinctive cantilevered design, painted in red. Supposedly when you have finished repainting it, it is time to start again at the other end.

Brexit looks like a Forth Bridge for UK based businesses – just when you think you have made preparations for whatever deal is done, a fresh round of negotiations and possible outcomes appear.

My database of all the Japanese companies in the UK is another Forth Bridge. Every time I think I have the definitive picture, I find more data to add. There is a free online government database, Companies House, to which all companies incorporated in the UK must submit their annual reports. If they are above a certain size, they must also give an account of the risks they face and what they are doing to mitigate them.

By reading these reports, I can cross check other records of employee numbers, turnover and capital. I can therefore say with some confidence that there are over 1000 Japan originated entities in the UK (including branches) and they employ over 160,000 people, with total turnover of around £100bn. I can also see what steps Japanese companies have taken to prepare for Brexit.

Much of this has been in the news already. Those companies who are physically moving products - whether in the automotive supply chain, or pharmaceuticals or electronics – have stockpiled, expanded their warehousing and reviewed their logistics. Those companies who are in regulated sectors such as finance or pharmaceuticals have strengthened their EU bases and made the necessary applications to EU authorities for approval for their services or products.

There have also been structural changes. Plenty of the larger Japanese companies were already in a holding company structure across Europe, with holding companies mostly in the UK, Netherlands or Germany. Electronics and trading companies are turning their UK companies into branches of EU holding companies, or turning their UK companies into "commission agents" so that the principal in a sales contract is in the EU. Some have reduced the capital they have in the UK.

This has not caused an immediate or dramatic negative impact on jobs, but in the long run I worry about the loss of influence and budget that this may have for UK business.

The mood at the Japanese Chamber of Commerce & Industry in the UK's New Year party in 2019 was very positive, however. The message of the speeches was that Japan and the UK have so many common interests, they need to stick together. Membership of the Chamber is at a record high as new Japanese companies continue to invest in the UK, largely in domestic oriented businesses such as food, retail or public sector outsourcing, symbolised by the stunning flower arrangement provided by Aoyama Flower Market, who opened their first UK branch in London in 2018.

13. SPAIN

I was initially surprised to see that Madrid scored highest amongst the European alternatives to post-Brexit London as a location for Japanese financial services companies, according to research from the Daiwa Institute. The obvious choices, Amsterdam and Frankfurt, were a close second, with Dublin and Paris trailing behind.

Most British people think of Spain as a holiday or retirement destination. Indeed, one of the reasons Madrid scored highly in the research was for its climate, recreational opportunities and a generally high standard of living, with lower prices.

Commercial property is also cheaper and more available in Madrid than other European financial capitals and as Spain has a large population of younger, well educated people, salaries are not as high as in London.

There are some drawbacks to setting up a business in Spain. The Daiwa Institute mentions the lack of English ability, but I would say in the financial services sector, this is probably not an issue, as many younger Spanish people have been travelling and working abroad over the past decade so are more willing to accept working in English, compared to the still strong "anti-Anglo" sentiment in France.

The aspect not mentioned by the Daiwa Institute, but which is of concern to most British I know who have businesses in Spain, is the bureaucracy and general ease of doing business. According to the World Bank, Spain scored 33 in 2015/6 (where 1= most business friendly), compared to 6 for the UK, 14 for Germany, 15 for Ireland, 27 for the Netherlands and 28 for France.

Although Spanish tax rates are low, the labour market is highly regulated, and was one of the causes of the tragically high youth unemployment rate of over 50% at peak, in the years after the 2008 economic crash. However, the unemployment rate is now at its lowest since 2009 and Spain's economy had one of the highest Eurozone growth rates last year.

As well as an improvement in the economy, Spain has not seen a rise of anti-immigrant, anti-EU, populist movements, unlike the other main EU economies. Only 10% of Spanish people support leaving the EU and although there have been large numbers of immigrants from Morocco and Romania, many Spanish people have also migrated and re-migrated over the past 10 years. Immigration in search of jobs is viewed as a perfectly natural behaviour and not a threat.

Spanish nationalism does not have much political appeal. It is negatively associated with the fascism of the Franco dictatorship, and the suppression of regional Catalan and Basque identities.

Many recent immigrants to Spain also came from Latin American countries, with similar language, religious beliefs and culture. This is the final reason that Spain could be attractive to Japanese companies – Spain is an obvious gateway to other growing economies – in Latin America and also - because of geographical proximity - northern Africa, where many Japanese automotive suppliers are opening factories.

14. A SECOND LOOK AT FRANCE

I wrote previously about the difficulties of doing business in France, especially the amount of bureaucracy that has to be dealt with. The new French government under Emmanuel Macron has been trying to overcome this image problem by promising to deregulate and lower taxes, particularly for banks. There have even been advertising campaigns promoting the charms of Paris in an attempt to lure banks from London post Brexit.

So far this does not seem to be working for Japanese banks and financial services companies, who are largely choosing either Frankfurt or Amsterdam for their post Brexit EU base and in any case look likely to keep their broader European or EMEA coordination functions in London.

Financial services companies need to be based near where their customers are, so it is not surprising Japanese banks would choose Germany or the Netherlands over France, and not move too much out of the UK for the time being, as there are far more large Japanese companies, regional headquarters, and also Japanese expatriate staff in the UK, Germany and the Netherlands than in France.

I found, through my researches, that the Japanese companies with substantial presence in France reflect France's traditional strengths of food and drink, imaging technology and fashion and beauty, along with automotive companies, which have a dominant presence across the EMEA region.

The EU Japan trade agreement and partnership will boost trade in the food and automotive sectors, so it may well be that more Japanese companies will be looking at France again and French companies will also be trying more actively to do business in Japan.

Nonetheless, I am very reluctant to have a registered company in France, even though it is becoming clear it will be difficult for us to provide training to our clients in France if I do not have a legal entity there.

My researches into Japanese companies in France also revealed that Sony has shrunk its French workforce considerably over the past few years and that reminded me of the incident where the Sony France CEO and HR director were held hostage overnight by the workers of a Sony factory that was being closed down.

France has a long tradition of striking, protest and direct confrontation between workers and employers and citizens and their government. This attitude also impacts the way they do business – the City of London Envoy to the EU described in a recent memo how shocked he was to discover in his meeting with Banque de France that the French wanted a hard, disruptive Brexit, even if it came at a cost to the EU overall, and saw the City of London as adversaries, not partners.

I am not at all surprised by this, nor was it particularly surprising to see French military, teachers and local authorities protesting about Macron's proposed cuts and deregulation. Strikes, demonstrations and blockades are part of business life in France.

15. POLAND, MIGRATION AND THE FUTURE OF THE EU

Polish immigrants represented the largest group of foreigners living in the UK for the first time in 2015. There were around 831,000 Polish born residents in the UK, overtaking Indian born residents. This represents a ¾ million increase on 2004 when Poland joined the EU, showing the scale and speed of the increase in immigrants from Eastern Europe – one of the root causes of the British vote to leave the EU.

Poland's connections to the UK go back further than this, however. A large group of Poles settled in the UK after WWII, and were welcomed because of the well-known heroism of Polish pilots who flew in the Battle of Britain.

Trading links with Poland date back even further, to medieval times and the Hanseatic League of merchants who did business with each other from Russia through the Baltics to Germany, the Low Countries and into the UK.

But it would be wrong to think of this as a European Union style alliance of nation states. League membership was by city. Many of the European countries as we know them now did not exist then. Member cities such as

Gdansk or the Hanse capital of Lübeck were semi-autonomous, or controlled by the Holy Roman Empire, or Prussia, or Denmark. And of course, more recently the eastern part was under the domain of Soviet communism.

If you visit Gdansk now, the old part of the city is in fact a beautiful, partly imaginary, post-war reconstruction of a pre-Germanic past. The actual old city had been obliterated by WWII. Also worth a visit is the European Solidarity Centre which commemorates the Gdansk shipyard union Solidarność and asserts that its strike in 1980/1 started the process which ended in the Berlin Wall coming down in 1989.

British people who are sceptical about the European Union say it should only be about trade, and that they want control back of UK borders, money and laws. For other EU members, the EU was a way of regaining control of their lives, by ensuring peace and democracy. This aim was not so appealing to the UK, who had no such recent experience of ground wars, dictatorships or being occupied by other countries.

Many people and political leaders in other EU member countries – including Poland – are beginning to say the EU represents a threat to their national sovereignty too. Border controls are being reinstated and there is a strong possibility eventually the EU itself will disintegrate.

Polish residents in the UK are worrying what will happen to them post Brexit and the millions of British who live elsewhere in the EU are also nervous for their future.

Many of the people working for Japanese companies in the EU are migrants, so I think the best thing Japanese companies can do right now is reassure them that they will look after them, and if necessary offer relocation to subsidiaries in other countries, including Japan.

16. BREXIT BUSINESS OPPORTUNITIES

A couple of Japanese expatriate business people with whom I was having lunch both remarked how surprised they were that their British colleagues were quick to recover from the Brexit shock and think positively about the business opportunities it might bring. I too had been trying to be positive and did some research into how Japanese companies are evolving in the UK. The opportunities I identified for Japanese companies in the UK were:

1. Africa and the Middle East

The UK has historic ties to Africa and the Middle East, which means that is still a good base for coordinating activities across those regions as there are many expatriates from and experts in those regions, who live in the UK, and are sources of information and management capability.

The UK government is going to be looking to boost trade to non-EU countries, as a counterbalance to any negative impact from Brexit on trade with the EU, so there is likely to be plenty of support for developing business with these regions.

It might even be easier than before to hire people from those regions in the UK. Although a vote for Brexit was partly to stop immigration to the UK, this was very much about preventing lower skilled people from Eastern Europe living in the UK. Most Japanese companies were not hiring such people in the first place, so I doubt any restrictions on this kind of immigration will have much impact.

Japanese financial services companies are already changing the status of non-UK branches to a European Union branch or incorporated subsidiary, and are strengthening their African operations, but it looks like those operations will still be reporting into the London office, which will act as an EMEA coordination function.

Japanese manufacturers have already shifted lower skilled, labour intensive production eastwards in Europe or to Africa and I assume Brexit will accelerate this trend, with the UK being a regional hub for engineering design and development expertise.

2. Infrastructure

Despite the fact that manufacturing has moved eastwards or south to Africa, the British government is well aware that British people desperately want well paid, secure manual worker jobs to return to the UK. The most obvious way to do this is through public sector investment in transportation and energy. Hitachi and other such infrastructure companies should still find plenty of business, although it is not clear what will happen to EU funding for energy and transport infrastructure projects.

3. Acquisitions in the UK

As Softbank's acquisition of ARM proved, there are still companies in the UK which are attractive acquisition targets, not as a gateway to the Single Market but because they are unique in terms of their brand, technology or expertise. For example, food and drink brands unique to the UK, Lloyds underwriters and UK advertising agencies have all recently been acquired by Japanese companies. It seems likely the weak pound and strong yen will continue for a while, so there may be some bargains for the brave.

17. AFRICA AND EMEA

Many Japanese companies have set up European regional headquarters, largely in the UK, Germany or the Netherlands and use this as a base for consolidating their administrative activities across the region. Increasingly these days the designated region covered is not just Europe, but EMEA – Europe, Middle East and Africa. The historical ties that the UK in particular has with Africa and the Middle East, means that it is not only easy to access the Middle East and Africa from London, but also that it is relatively easy to get hold of information about countries in those regions in the UK as there are many expatriates and experts on those countries based in the UK.

One such expert is Professor Sir Paul Collier, a professor of economics at Oxford University, whose speech to a group of Japanese businesspeople in London I attended a while back. Sir Paul had met Shinzo Abe at a G8 meeting, and his speech was largely in support of the recent initiatives by Abe and Japanese businesses to become more involved in Africa, recently reinforced by the TICAD meeting in Nairobi.

He was realistic, however, saying that "I am not going to tell you Africa is wonderful. Africa is complicated and has a small economy, but it has got significant opportunities." The opportunities fall into four main areas – natural resources, the infrastructure needed to exploit those resources, growth in sectors such as electric power, construction, consumer goods and the "e-economy" such as payments by mobile phone.

He also pointed to the specific attractions that Africa would have for Japan. Firstly, that as African growth is very commodity price dependent, and Japan is a big commodity importer, having investments in Africa is a useful "hedge" against commodity price movements. Secondly, Japan is apparently welcome in Africa. "Africa is tired of Europe and doesn't like being told what to do". The USA behaves like a colonial power but does not have any money to invest into Africa. China was hugely popular in Africa 10 years ago, but apparently many African leaders are now feeling frightened of becoming too dependent on China and are trying to push back on deals.

The biggest negative for Japan, in Sir Paul's opinion, is that culturally, "Africa is Japan upside down. Japanese society is one of very high trust and very high social cohesion, and Africa isn't". And of course, Africa isn't one country, but 54 countries and the levels of opportunities and risk vary considerably from one country to another. Sir Paul's recommendations were to focus on Lagos and Nairobi, with possibly a sub office in Rwanda. With regard to corruption, the risk is reputational rather than financial, and he recommends having a policy and making it very clear to counterparts what that policy is.

He also reinforced the view that approaching Africa from the UK was a good tactic. "The UK, public and private sectors, have the knowledge, network and the contacts but not the products that Africa wants." Japan has those products, so, teaming up with the British should bring plenty of mutual benefit.

18. ARE JAPAN AND TURKEY CULTURALLY SIMILAR?

I decided to use the excuse of the Istanbul location of the annual conference of the Association of Japanese Studies to visit Turkey for the first time in July 2013. This was long overdue for me as not only is Istanbul the place to see where East meets West, straddling as it does Europe and Asia, but I had noticed many of my Japanese clients were expanding their business in Turkey recently. This is confirmed by the fact that bilateral trade between Japan and Turkey rose 25% in 2012, reaching a record $4.6bn, and there are now 120 Japanese companies with offices in Turkey as of 2013.

The day before the conference opened, Toyota started production of its new Corolla model at its Turkey plant. I had dinner that evening with my Turkish business school friend, now heading up a successful private equity firm in Turkey. He was well aware of Toyota's activities but also expressed some concern over the announcement that a Japanese consortium was going to build a nuclear power plant in Turkey.

If Japanese companies are going to move more into these kinds of infrastructure projects, in Turkey and elsewhere in Europe, then harmonious relationships with consortium partners and local governments will be critical. Judging by the interactions I saw between the Turkish Ambassador to the UK and senior Japanese business people in London recently, relationships are cordial so far, despite rivalry over the 2020 Olympics.

Turkish people I have spoken to who have worked with Japanese people tell me that Japanese and Turkish colleagues communicate well with each other, which is good to hear, although it could mean there is not much business opportunity for my company.

There is some evidence that the Turkish and Japanese languages are historically related. Both are "WYSIWYG" (What You See Is What You Get) languages – pronounced as they are spelt, with each syllable clearly enunciated, unlike English with its deceptive spellings and elisions. Apparently Turkish is also grammatically similar to Japanese, with the verb coming towards the end of the sentence, and plenty of scope for vagueness and distancing or removing the subject from the sentence.

It turns out that Turkish people are more used to the apprenticeship style of learning too, rather than formal, classroom-based training –

similar to the Japanese *"minitsukeru"* [which literally means "stick on the flesh"] way of learning. Again, this may work well in manufacturing environments, but I wonder whether in situations where more peer to peer, management communication is needed, for example between the partners of an infrastructure project, differences in communication and decision-making style might not become more apparent. So maybe there will be a business chance for my company there.

19. SIMILARITIES BETWEEN ARAB AND JAPANESE CULTURES

An Arab participant in one of my seminars in Dubai in 2018 suddenly put up her hand and blurted out, "I recognise this so well in my family!" when I was describing Japanese group orientation and non-verbal communication and concepts such as *"ishindenshin"* and *"omoiyari"*.

I asked in what way she thought Arab people and Japanese people were similar, and she told me that three generations of her family live together, just as traditional Japanese families used to. One evening, her grandmother asked her "what are you thinking of eating this evening?" The young woman was actually about to go and get a McDonalds hamburger, but recognising that her grandmother was hungry, asked her what she would like to eat. Her grandmother said "oh I am not hungry. I don't need anything."

So the young women went to buy a take away traditional Arab meal. When she offered it to her grandmother, her grandmother refused it. They started to eat, leaving a portion with her grandmother, who then finally started to eat it.

This is not the first time I have been told by an Arab person that Japanese and Arab cultures have a lot of similarities. When I ask why, they mention a mix of family orientation, a strong relationship orientation in business, respect for seniors, and, as the young woman's story about her grandmother illustrated, being very indirect in expressing needs.

You would think then, that it might be easy for a Japanese person to fit into the Arab business culture, but actually there are two issues for the many Japanese expatriates working in Dubai that make this less easy. One is that Dubai itself is one of the most multicultural cities in the world. 88% of the population are not Emirati. Almost everyone is a guest worker rather than having permanent residency. So Japanese expatriates in my workshop had to cope with many nationalities on their team, ranging from Europeans to Indians to Lebanese.

Secondly, group orientation means that there is a clear sense of in-group and out-group. Expatriates in Dubai find it very hard to become an "insider" in Dubai society. For example, amongst Arab business people, during Ramadan, it is customary to visit customers' houses in the evening for the meal which breaks the fast. Hospitality is another very strong cultural value in Arab culture. Nonetheless, I can imagine you would have to be a very brave person to turn up at a customer's house if you weren't an Arab yourself.

So Japanese companies have done the sensible thing, which is to hire young local Arab graduates, offering them training and a career paths. However, there is huge diversity even amongst Arabs. Sitting next to the headscarf wearing woman who told me about her grandmother was the other graduate recruit, another young woman, wearing an abaya (traditional Arab dress), but with her long hair uncovered. She had been educated at an international school, and felt more close to the American cultural values I described.

20. SERVICE OR SERVICES?

A Japanese entrepreneur told me that his friends tried to discourage him from setting up a services company, because - they said - "Japanese customers won't pay for service". He said this in Japanese, and I assumed he meant "services" in the plural, which in English means work that would be included in the "service sector" of the economy, in other words not the agricultural or manufacturing sectors.

That really struck a chord with me, as I also sell "services" - namely consulting and training - to Japanese companies and I have occasionally noticed that Japanese people seem reluctant to pay for what we do. Despite this, I have had a profitable business for 15 years, probably because my actual client contacts at those Japanese companies are usually Europeans, and Europeans are much more accustomed to pay for consulting and training.

There is a translation issue here, because If in English, we use "service" without the "a" or use "the" instead – for example "pay for service", or "how was the service?" we mean customer service. So I think that is where the confusion lies. Maybe what the entrepreneur's friends were saying is that Japanese customers are not prepared to pay additionally for customer service. It is assumed in Japan that good customer service is automatic, and part of what you are already paying for.

How a concept is translated into another language often provides a clue as to how that concept is viewed in that culture. Particularly with Japanese, if the word only exists in *katakana*, the alphabet used for borrowed foreign words, that may mean that concept does not really exist in Japan. And サービス(sa-bisu) in Japanese not only means "service" in English, but has an additional meaning of being "a free thing".

How to charge for a service is more complicated than charging for a product. It is a mixture of the hours involved and the expertise being bought. A potential customer once told me that my company's training was 50% more expensive than another supplier (whose main business was a language school). I said that this was the price we charged to customers in a similar situation to them and it was fair value for the expertise we had. I knew the language school would not have that expertise and indeed the customer ultimately chose us, despite our higher cost.

Above all, customers in Europe are willing to pay for services which solve a problem they have. Just telling them how high quality something is or how expert you are or how many hours it takes is not enough. This is why sales people for B2B services companies in Europe first of all try to build up trust with customers so they will tell them what their problems are. And also why it is more fashionable to use the word "solution" rather than "service" – this word implies they are getting an integrated product and service, which will fix a problem that they have.

21. TECHNOLOGY AND SERVICE

I asked two Japanese expatriates who were both on their second stint in the UK what had changed since their last stay in the UK 10 or so years' ago. To my surprise, both said that they thought customer service had improved.

My initial response was that this was probably due to the big increase in people from Eastern Europe who are working as waiters, shop assistants and so on, with far more enthusiasm and efficiency than had been normal in the UK in the past.

But on discussing this further, and thinking about my own recent experiences, I realise the improvement they were talking about has more to do with technology than the cultural mindset of service sector employees. One of the Japanese expatriates noted that "when you arrange for someone to come to your house to repair something, they arrive when they say they will". This used not to be the case – you could take a whole day off work waiting for someone and not even get a phone call explaining the delay.

When I recently bought a washing machine, I purchased it online and chose a time slot and a day for it to be delivered. I was surprised to see that they would deliver up until 21:00 in the evening. Then followed a series of emails and text messages from the store to remind me and offer me a chance to change the slot if I wanted. It's common to receive further texts during the day of delivery, narrowing the time slot down to within one hour. The delivery and trades people have some kind of handheld GPS device which helps them map their journeys from customer to customer and they can be tracked and assisted by support staff in their company offices.

Then, this week, I realised another item I had bought from Amazon had not arrived, so I went online, clicked the "call me" button and within 1 second someone (I suspect from an Indian call centre) called my mobile phone and immediately arranged for a replacement to be sent the next day.

I realise this kind of service is available in other countries, but it does seem according to various surveys that the British are the biggest online shoppers in the world. According to McKinsey, although internet penetration is higher in the US that Europeans, Europeans are much more likely to prefer a digital channel for buying or using banking services than Americans.

Services now account for 80% of the UK economy, so it's no surprise I suppose that the UK has got better at delivering them. For Japanese companies, despite Brexit, the British service sector still represents an investment opportunity – both to gain technology and to reach other virtual markets in the rest of the world. It is noticeable that recent acquisitions or investments into the UK from Japan have largely been in the technology-based services sector– from Softbank acquiring ARM, through to Aioi Nissay Dowa acquiring InsuretheBox.

22. DATA VISUALISATION

I often advise Europeans who are trying to communicate a proposal, or want to have a discussion with Japanese counterparts, to try to put their idea into a visual format. This has several benefits. One is that it should reduce the amount of English text that the Japanese person has to plough through to understand what is being proposed. A second reason is that it depersonalizes the discussion if there is a graphical representation – a "thing" that can be pointed at and disagreed with during the argument, rather than having to argue with someone's abstract idea.

Thirdly, Japanese written language – kanji – is highly graphical as a communication method, so Japanese people are more receptive to complex concepts being communicated in a graphical and holistic way rather than the textual, linear form common in the West.

I was quite surprised therefore to hear a young Japanese expatriate woman tell me that her colleagues in the UK based market research agency she works for are much more accustomed to representing their findings in a graphical way than she was used to in Japan. Specifically, she said that they use infographics and sometimes even send the report to clients as a video, using the infographics and clips of customers being interviewed.

With the advent of "Big Data", data visualization is a growing industry. So should Japanese companies be acquiring companies or hiring people who have those skills, or is this another area which will simply be automated, and all that is needed is to buy in or develop some software?

Automation tools already exist for data visualization, but the key is to think about why you want to put the data into a visual format in the first place. It is usually to give insights which will then provoke a discussion. An infographic does not of itself provide the solution. Discussions require human beings to provide their different interpretations of the infographics and ideas about how to act on them. The infographic provides the "thing" that can be pointed at and disagreed with, but also allows people of diverse backgrounds and native languages to have a more equal chance of contributing to the debate, because there is less of a language or technical barrier.

The market research agency at which the Japanese woman worked was founded in the UK and acquired by a Japanese company in 2014. But it also has offices across Asia, multinational staff who travel across Europe and a call centre based in the UK covering over 30 languages.

The UK is the obvious location for global marketing services, not just because it is the home of English language communication, but because of its multinational workforce, who can ensure the data is interpreted appropriately for different cultures. This is why Japanese marketing and advertising agencies have been acquiring many British companies recently. I just hope Brexit does not damage this advantage by putting up too many barriers to immigration and free movement across Europe.

23. FOOD HYBRIDIZATION BETWEEN EUROPE AND JAPAN

The EU-Japan Economic Partnership Agreement (EPA) has been characterised in Europe as "cars for cheese". As a cheese loving North European, I did indeed miss being able to buy reasonably priced good quality cheese when I was living in Japan. It was a kind of comfort food for me – either hunks of cheese on bread, or sometimes I would have what I called my "spaghetti Bolognese" moment, where I would crave the *umami* of a tomato and beef sauce smothered with parmesan cheese.

But because I also lived in Japan as a child, traditional Japanese foods are comfort food for me too. Now I am living in the UK – I sometimes make miso soup (particularly the red miso I remember from when I was a child in Sendai), or *okonomiyaki*, or curry rice or *tonkatsu* to cheer myself up.

The EPA now has to be approved by various local European parliaments, and one of the ways of persuading them to accept the agreement is to point out that it will ensure the geographical designation of over 200 European food and drink products are protected in the Japanese market, such as Polish vodka or Parma ham.

If this argument is sufficiently persuasive to local parliaments, the agreement is expected to be ratified in 2018 and implemented in 2019.

Europeans get very passionate about the authenticity of local food – particularly the Italians. There is even a Twitter account called "Italians mad at food" (@Italiancomments) which retweets comments from Italians outraged – mostly at Americans – for putting mushrooms or garlic in carbonara sauce or pineapple on pizza.

Italians would not be impressed with my spaghetti Bolognese either – there is no such dish as spaghetti Bolognese in Italy. There is ragu alla Bolognese, which means simply a meat sauce – and is meant to be eaten with tagliatelle, not spaghetti.

The British have a long history of adopting foods from other cultures – our favourite national dish is Chicken Tikka Masala – which is a curry which does not exist in India – and the second or third generation British

Chinese who run our takeaway food shops have become resigned to putting sweet and sour sauce on fries.

The British have become far more sophisticated about foreign food these days. Multicultural street food has become fashionable across Europe – most major cities have markets full of *"yatai"* (food stalls)– one in my town has a Chilean stall and a falafel stall which is actually run by a couple of Koreans.

Japanese people are somewhat dismayed to see fast food chains selling "sushi" in the UK which have little resemblance to the authentic Japanese version but of course curry rice, tempura and tonkatsu are actually hybrid Japanese/European/Indian foods themselves.

So the EPA seems likely to herald another chapter of hybridization. Japan and Europe will trade in each other's authentic, local foods, and create new hybrids that will be the comfort foods for the next generation. It's a business opportunity both for traditional farmers and adventurous cooks.

24. BREXIT ACCELERATES EXISTING TRENDS

The election in the UK in 2017 undoubtedly increased the possibility of a softer Brexit - and maybe even that Brexit will not happen at all. Various senior British politicians became more outspoken in their opposition to a "hard" Brexit of leaving the Single Market without any deal and defaulting to WTO rules. The French President Emmanuel Macron and the German Finance Minister Wolfgang Schäuble both said that they would support the UK should it wish to stay in the EU after all.

There were calls for businesses in the UK to be bolder in their demands to protect their supply chains and to be able to hire and relocate employees within the EU as they wish and there were signals the British government may be more open to such suggestions from business than previously.

What should Japanese companies in the UK do next? The Japanese government was quite outspoken from the outset about Japanese companies wanting the UK to retain as many of the benefits of EU membership as possible. Japanese businesses could now try to join with other multinationals in the UK to put further pressure on the UK government to go for the most business and job friendly deal, or even stay in the EU.

But I suspect that the damage is already done. A soft Brexit may not be technically feasible and would always be a worse deal than staying in the EU, so businesses and employees have been preparing for the worst-case scenario already.

We are already seeing the impact of this – net immigration to the UK is starting to fall. For example, the number of non-British EU applications to become nurses in the UK dropped 96% from 2016 to 2017. Anecdotally I have heard that EU citizens working in the UK have already started to leave and smaller businesses with EU customers have relocated entirely from the UK to other European countries.

I doubt larger multinationals are going to move their whole operations out of the UK, but they have already started transferring people and parts of their business to the continent, particularly to Germany. Apparently, this is already resulting in labour shortages in Germany, so we are now seeing advertisements from German recruitment agencies who specialise in Japanese speakers in Japanese language magazines on sale in the UK.

I meet up from time to time with other UK business owners who supply services to Japanese companies – legal, recruitment, translation and research. At our most recent meeting it became apparent that we are all making similar changes to our approach. For services, it doesn't matter so much where you are located, and our customers are increasingly asking for regional or global services, so we are staying in the UK for the time being, but being much more aggressive in marketing our services outside of the UK - not just in Europe, but also Japan and Asia.

Brexit is accelerating trends that were already underway, whether it actually happens or not.

25. EXPORTING OMOTENASHI

It was a very tough few months for high street retail in the UK and elsewhere at the beginning of 2018. Supermarkets, clothing brands and electronics all had casualties in the UK. As always, the disruptive effect of eCommerce is blamed. Rumours are swirling that even the UK upmarket supermarket chain Waitrose has been approached by Amazon as an acquisition prospect.

So maybe this is a good moment for Japanese retail and ecommerce companies to make another attempt to expand overseas, after the relative failure of Rakuten. Clearly Mercari thinks so, announcing alongside its IPO that will increase its investments in the US market, aiming to be the first Japanese start up to make it in the USA.

But rather than go down the disruptive route of simply undercutting prices online, I wonder whether Japanese companies could be more innovative in the service they provide, and find ways to bring the famous Japanese value of *omotenashi* (usually translated as "hospitality") to the world.

I shopped at the Cos (a Swedish mid-market brand from the same company as H&M) flagship store in Regent's Street in London recently. It was full of Chinese tourists but also local people, trying on piles of clothes. It was not a pleasant experience and most of the clothes had cosmetics stains on them. I wondered why anyone would buy anything and then realised that what the local people were doing was trying, and then buying the clothes online.

This makes it difficult to incentivise the shop assistants to give good service or keep the shop environment pleasant either through commission or through positive feedback, as there is little direct sense of achievement or impact on sales. But of course the physical customer experience has become even more crucial now if retailers with high street presence are to compete with pure online retailers.

This point was reinforced by the speaker at my local business women's network. She has started an upmarket women's fashion brand - £500 for vibrantly coloured, tailor-made dresses in Italian wool. It is a highly personal service and she says that she has also discovered that customers are willing to pay simply to spend an hour and a half with her.

We did wonder why she had made the effort to travel 2 hours to talk to us for free, considering we might not be rich enough to afford her dresses. And she was also kind enough to give me some free careers advice afterwards. I suppose it links back to what she said in her speech about one of her core values being to give, without expecting to receive anything back, at least at first. This is the deeper meaning of *omotenashi*. Not just "hospitality" but a selfless giving, which is why Japanese customer service is world famous.

I know some Japanese clothing companies like Start Today are trying to replicate excellent personalised service online. It would be great if Japanese companies in other sectors could do this physically as well as online outside of Japan. The UK certainly has plenty of empty shops available.

26. SUMMER EXHIBITION

The Summer Exhibition at the Royal Academy is an annual art exhibition and one of the events of the London Season, a summer of parties and events such as the Chelsea Flower Show, the Epsom Derby and the Henley Royal Regatta.

You might expect the Summer Exhibition to be very traditionally British, but this year, to mark the 250th anniversary of the Summer Exhibition, the not very traditional, self-described "transvestite potter" Grayson Perry was asked to curate the exhibition, on a larger, more diverse and inclusive scale than ever before.

Just as in previous years, the members of the Royal Academy - professional artists - exhibit their recent work at the exhibition and non-members were also invited to submit works of art. Perry and his team viewed a record 20, 000 works for selection and as a result the rooms were crammed with all kinds of paintings, sculptures, videos, embroideries and architectural models created by people of many nationalities, including some Japanese artists such as Katsutoshi Yuasa.

It could have been an incoherent mess, but actually I think it succeeded in capturing the UK right now: creative, humorous, political, multicultural, celebrating the amateurish and the outsider, but also the British countryside, cityscapes and people.

Before visiting the exhibition, I attended a lunch at which a British trade minister spoke. He was trying to be positive about Brexit, emphasising that the UK would continue to be a good place to invest because of our excellent research-oriented universities, skilled and creative workforce and stable legal and financial infrastructure. He pointed out that NTT Data and Fujitsu have both invested in UK based technology initiatives in the past year.

He did not of course mention that manufacturing operations in the automotive supply chain are beginning to shift to the EU. Jaguar Land Rover announced it will move production to Slovakia, which is also where at least one Japanese automotive components supplier with production in the UK has set up a plant in the last year.

Most of the questions from the audience of Japan-related business people were about immigration however. The cap for visas for non-EU immigrants (which includes Japanese intra company transfers) has been reached every month for the past 6 months and EU immigrants have started returning to their home countries or not coming to the UK in the first place.

UK unemployment is at a historic low. One Japanese recruitment agency told me that their UK vacancies have increased 50% year on year. Firms are worried that after Brexit it will become even more difficult to recruit EU and non-EU workers.

One proposed solution, which will take some time, is to train low skilled British people in higher levels of skills and replace low skilled labour with robotics. But as the Summer Exhibition proved, diversity and multicultural influences are what have defined and made the UK an attractive place for innovation in the first place.

27. HARD BREXIT ALTERNATIVES FOR SERVICES

The UK government's "soft" Brexit proposal, to allow freedom of movement of goods between the UK and the EU, is unlikely to be acceptable by the EU or even a practical solution for the UK economy. It's politically understandable why the government is trying to protect the just-in-time delivery of manufacturing supply chains, in which many Japanese companies are involved. The manufacturing regions mainly voted in favour of leaving the EU. It might be possible to persuade those voters to accept a soft Brexit if they realise their jobs are under threat from a hard Brexit. But 80% of the UK economy is in the services sector – predominantly in cities and in the south east, where the vote was largely to remain in the EU.

It's not so easy these days, however, to make a distinction between services and manufacturing for the purposes of customs checks and regulatory compliance, even in the car industry. 10% of Nissan's workforce in the UK work in a technology design centre in the south east, not in the factory in the north east, developing software and services, not just components for cars.

Fujitsu, the largest employer in the UK, may be a manufacturer in Japan, but only provides IT services in the UK. The number of Fujitsu staff in the UK has been falling over the past few years, whereas it has been increasing in Global Delivery Centres in Portugal and Poland. Fujitsu is now the largest Japanese employer in Portugal – employing around 1000 people who provide technical support to global customers by phone and internet.

Both Poland and Portugal can provide the low cost, multilingual, well-educated workforces needed by the services sector. Although it is not a big market in its own right, the Portuguese economy has recovered since the euro zone crisis – the budget deficit is the lowest in 40 years, the unemployment rate has improved and it is politically stable.

For my own business, as an insurance against a "hard Brexit" for services, I might register for "e-residency" in Estonia. This will allow me to set up a company in Estonia and open a euro denominated bank account there so we can easily send and receive euros, within the eurozone. It will also allow me - under EU data protection regulation and the new deal with Japan - to share client data freely with my colleagues in the EU and in Japan.

Similarly, any UK based companies in strongly regulated sectors such as financial and legal services are making sure they have credible presence in the EU, so they can continue to do business there.

Nobody is expecting the service export sector to move entirely away from the UK if there is a hard Brexit. Alternatives to the UK have other disadvantages – political instability in Eastern Europe, or high costs and scarcity of good office locations and employees in Western Europe – but I predict this current trend of dispersed locations across Europe will accelerate.

AFTERWORD

THE PARALLEL DEVELOPMENT OF EUROVISION AND THE EUROPEAN UNION

Giving the Japanese version of this book the title "Eurovision" was, I suppose, a typically British joke – "tongue in cheek" as we say. Most Europeans will immediately think of the Eurovision Song Contest – an annual televised singing competition, a bit like the *Kōhaku Uta Gassen*, a televised song contest on Japan's NHK TV channel that has happened every New Year since 1951.

There were two reasons for choosing this title. One is that there are various parallels between the Eurovision Song Contest and the European Union, which explain some of the issues around defining what Europe is. The second reason is that to be trusted in a complex, changing Europe, it is necessary to have a "vision" and to communicate it effectively to employees and customers.

Just like the European Union, the Eurovision Song Contest has been evolving for over 60 years. It started in 1956, with seven nations participating, for a very specific purpose – the Italian TV channel RAI had the agreement of European Broadcasting Union to organise and broadcast the contest, to test the limits of live broadcasting.

The EU started in 1951 with the Treaty of Paris, establishing the European Steel and Coal Community and the European Court of Justice, with 6 nations as members, with the specific purpose of integrating the steel and coal industries of those countries, particularly in the borderlands between France, Germany and the Benelux countries, to prevent future wars from breaking out again in the region.

Both the European Union and Eurovision have expanded their purpose since, evolving their rules and organisation accordingly. The purpose of the European Union is to promote the values of tolerance, respect for rules and democracy, to ensure that trust is built up between the member nations.

With the Treaties of Rome in 1957, the European Economic Community and the European Atomic Energy Community were established. Then the three communities were merged, with one commission, in the 1960s. In 1986 the Single European Act paved the way for the Single Market, and in 1992 the Maastricht Treaty was signed, established the European Union and giving greater say to the European Parliament.

More members joined the EU over the decades, most recently in 2013, when Croatia joined. Although initially France, under de Gaulle, opposed the UK joining, in 1973 Denmark, Ireland and the UK acceded and since then the European Union has expanded to 28 members. The conditions for joining are political (stable institutions, democracy, rule of law, human rights, respect for and protection of minorities), economic (functioning market economy, capacity to cope with competition and market forces) and administrative and institutional (capacity to implement the existing regulations of the EU and take on the obligations of membership).

There is nothing historical, religious or geographical in these conditions – which is why Muslim countries such as Turkey can apply to join.

Similarly, there are now over 40 countries competing in the Eurovision Song Contest, including Morocco and Australia. The rules have changed over the decades, particularly around qualification, voting and scoring. Other rules have remained constant such as the song must be no longer than 3 minutes, must be an original composition and cannot be purely instrumental.

Just like the EU, there are plenty of arguments amongst the countries participating in the Eurovision song contest regarding the rules which are more political in nature, particularly around what language – native language or English – can be used. Political feelings also become very apparent during the scoring process – countries which are friendly towards each other vote for each other and don't vote for those with whom they have difficulties. The UK has been in the bottom few scores in the finals for quite a few years now.

The UK does not take the Eurovision Song Contest seriously – rarely sending any of its more famous and talented popstars. The TV programme in the UK showing the contest is hosted by celebrities who mock all the contests sarcastically, knowing that most of the British viewers are drinking and laughing along with them.

Some British people asked, half seriously, if the UK would be thrown out of the Eurovision Song Contest if it left the EU. Scare stories and myths about the EU have been promoted by the British media for decades - for example that the EU insists on straight not bendy bananas - so some people were willing to believe that this could happen.

But as well as mocking what they see as the sillier aspects of the EU, those in favour of the UK leaving the EU often cite the need to regain sovereignty. In particular, they object to the principle of the freedom of movement of people, especially the large numbers who came into the UK from the more recent member countries.

Those who are most vehemently against the European Union think the real vision and purpose of the European Union is to create a Germany dominated super-state. But actually, the UK has been very instrumental in both developing the rules and regulations in the first place, and also promoting EU enlargement. The idea was that enlargement would weaken German and French influence, and the rules and regulations needed British influence, to prevent too much corporatism and promote free trade.

Although British people generally were and still are in favour of the free trade aspects of the EU, it's clear that many were never fully signed up to the values and vision of the European Union as a way to avoid further wars. It may be because the UK never suffered a land war either in World War I or World War II the way Germany, France and the Benelux countries did. Instead, many British, particularly the older generations, have a positive, nostalgic view of the Second World War, where Britain stood alone, British people were united in fighting the evils of Nazi Germany, enduring air bombing and food rationing and ultimately liberating France and the rest of Europe (conveniently forgetting the role that the USA and Soviet Union had in this).

Successive British governments have not sold the vision or the values of the European Union, preferring instead to expend energy on gaining all kinds of opt outs from various European Union initiatives such as the Schengen Area (crossing borders without passports), joining the euro, and justice and home affairs legislation.

I worry that Japanese companies may end up falling into the same trap in Europe. There is a tendency in Japanese companies to worry far too much about the rules of doing business, and following processes, without thinking about the principles and the values behind these rules and processes. These principles and values need to form an appealing package along with the vision of the company, and need to be communicated very clearly, in order to make sure European employees, customers and partners are fully engaged.

STORY TELLING

Nations and companies need stories. Wally Olins, mentioned in the introduction of this book, created brands for countries as well as companies – including European countries such as Poland, Portugal and Lithuania. His point was that you cannot change perceptions of countries (or companies) just by good advertising, the brand has to be developed from truths about the country or company.

Therefore, you first of all have to ask questions of and listen to customers, employees and other stakeholders, to understand their perceptions of your brand. This is what the corporate brand office and global marketing team of which I was a member did at Fujitsu, with Wally Olins' guidance. We also then went on to develop stories, based on the real-life experiences of employees, which were compiled into a book[4] and we recorded videos of various executives talking about their experiences and encouraged them to make personalised speeches at conferences.

---

[4] Fortune Favors the Brave: The Fujitsu Way, *Kyoko Katase & Atsushi Tajima*, (Nikkei Business Publications: 2012)

I believe this way of communicating is well suited to Japanese companies and executives. Japanese employees know plenty of stories from the past, and because they have been working in the company for many decades, these stories have a strong personal flavour to them. There is an authenticity and a humility to many Japanese corporate stories that comes across very powerfully. I have touched on some of them in the articles in this book.

In fact, now I come to think of it, most of the articles in this book are actually stories, rather than a string of facts, because I think this makes them more appealing to the reader. I also tell many stories in my seminars as I know these are things people will remember, more than any facts about Japanese or European history or geography or theories of intercultural difference.

THE JAPANESE FAMILY STYLE COMPANY

I do however use one model to explain corporate cultures, developed by Fons Trompenaars and Charles Hampden-Turner.[5] They have developed a matrix, based on degree of hierarchy and degree of task versus relationship orientation, to outline four corporate cultures – the Guided Missile, The Eiffel Tower, the Incubator and the Family.

Guided Missiles are typical American, sales-oriented organisations where the communication is very direct and mainly around targets, deliverables, achievement, reward and bonus.

The **Eiffel Tower** organisation is more hierarchical, focused on structure. Communication is cascade style, from the top of the hierarchy, layer by layer to the bottom. People want to know about their status in the company, so worry about organisation charts and reporting lines, but they also want to know about the strategic direction. Where is the company going, and how can I contribute to this, and thereby be promoted? Just being given a target and told to hit it, is not enough.

---

[5]Riding the Waves of Culture: Understanding Cultural Diversity in Business, *Fons Trompenaars & Charles Hampden Turner*, (Nicholas Brearley: 2003), 159

Many people in Europe are used to the Eiffel Tower style of company and when they join a Japanese company, they are concerned by the lack of clear paths to progress their career and also a lack of clear, strategic direction.

Other Europeans in Japanese companies, particularly in the R&D, creative, IT, design engineering sectors are more used to the **Incubator** type of company. Here the main motivation is not money or status, but rather using one's skills and experience to make a difference and innovate. Structures and targets are necessary, but the communication needs to be authentic and management needs to be sympathetic to the needs of creative people.

Most Japanese companies belong to the **Family** style company. Even if they are not actually run by the founding family any more, they behave like a family. Despite all the changes that have happened over the past two decades in Japan, many of the bigger Japanese companies who are present in Europe, still have seniority-based pay (just like pocket money for children), lifetime employment (because you cannot fire members of the family) and an ethos of preserving the family name.

Japanese companies are appealing to Europeans partly because they are different. Many Europeans, particularly those who feel happiest in an "incubator" style company feel constricted or bored by the Eiffel Tower and Guided Missile style of operating.

It is therefore difficult for Family style companies to motivate employees with money or status, as these are dependent on seniority, rather than performance. Japanese companies in Europe have a reputation for good benefits, but only average pay, and also a sense that there is a limit to how far you can be promoted if you are not Japanese, in other words a family member.

There are some exceptions to this of course – Panasonic, Toyota, and Sony all have senior executives who are European. I think it is no accident that these companies are originally manufacturers, with innovative technologies.

These companies also have some good stories, usually about the founder and their philosophies. By finding ways to tell those stories to all employees around the world, they can feel like members of the family, who are familiar and connected with the with the company history, myths and key figures.

JAPANESE VALUES AND STRONG BRANDS

The other aspect that unites Panasonic, Toyota and Sony that they have strong brands. They are regularly the only Japanese brands that appear in global top 100 rankings.

But all of them have had challenges and I am sure all of those companies would say they have had to rethink and evolve their brands continually. Values cannot just be vague, feel good statements – they have to be something that employees can relate to their daily working lives. They have to be "actionable".

Other Japanese multinationals are facing the challenge of creating a distinctive brand in Europe and elsewhere and will no doubt face the same problem we faced at Fujitsu. The values that make Japanese companies trusted and admired by Europeans – high quality craftsmanship, collaborative with suppliers, responsive to customers and good corporate citizens mean that each company's mission statement and values come out sounding alike. "Contributing to society through innovation" could be the translation for many of them.

It was much easier for me to write press releases and other marketing material at Fujitsu once we had distilled our values into "genuine, responsive and ambitious", coming together in the vision "shaping tomorrow with you." It meant that any press release I wrote had to be about a genuine product or solution that actually existed, rather than was what is known in the IT industry as "vapourware". We had to show that it was in response to an actual customer need, and we had to give some idea of the future direction that Fujitsu was heading towards with this innovation. It meant our press releases were more of a story than a list of product specifications.

Some of the Japanese companies I now work with, particularly in the financial services sector, have incorporated the concept of "trust" into their vision and values. Given the damage done to the reputation of many Western banks by their behaviour leading up to the financial crisis of 2008/9, this is an understandable pitch to make.

Despite the string of recent corporate scandals, Japan and Japanese companies are still very trusted in Europe. More work needs to be done however, on the five elements of trust I mentioned in the introduction, particularly on the final link in the cycle, where vision and values are communicated clearly to employees, partners and customers.

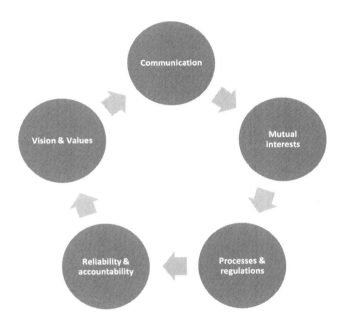

The five elements of building trust across cultures

For more details on what my company offers to support this, please visit www.rudlinconsulting.com

EUROPEAN TIMELINE & EUROPEAN UNION MEMBERS

EUROPEAN TIMELINE

800 BC to 146 BC	Ancient Greece
27BC	Roman Empire founded
395 AD	Roman Empire splits into Western and Eastern
476 AD	Western Roman Empire ends
476-800	Dark Ages
800-1000	Viking Age (raids on Western and Eastern Europe)
1066	Norman Conquest of England, Norman domination of Europe
1095-1291	The Crusades (religious wars in the Eastern Mediterranean)
1300-1600	Renaissance
1337-1453	Hundred Years' War (France vs England)
1517-1648	Protestant Reformation
1585-1604	Anglo-Spanish War
1618-1648	Thirty Years' War (Anti Habsburg/Protestant states vs Habsburg/Holy Roman Empire Catholic states)
1649	English Civil War ends in execution of Charles I of England & Scotland
1650-1800	Age of Enlightenment
1789-1799	French Revolution
1800-1900	Industrial Revolution
1803-1815	Napoleonic Wars
1914-1918	World War I
1917	Russian Revolution
1922-1923	Irish Civil War & Irish Free State
1929-1939	Great Depression
1936-1939	Spanish Civil War
1939-1945	World War II
1951	Treaty of Paris, European Steel and Coal Community between West Germany, France, Benelux, Italy
1957	Treaties of Rome, European Economic Community, European Atomic Energy Community
1960	European Free Trade Association formed (UK, Sweden,

	Denmark, Austria, Portugal, Norway, Switzerland)
1973	UK, Denmark and Ireland join EEC
1974	Carnation Revolution in Portugal, end of dictatorship
1975	Death of General Franco of Spain, end of military dictatorship
1986	Single European Act
1988-90	Strikes in Poland, fall of the Berlin Wall, Velvet Revolution in Czechoslovakia, Romanian Revolution, German reunification
1992	Maastricht Treaty – establishment of European Union
1999	Euro currency introduced
2004	A10 enlargement of European Union (Cyprus, the Czech Republic, Estonia, Hungary, Latvia, Lithuania, Malta, Poland, Slovakia, and Slovenia)
2009-	Eurozone crisis
2016	British referendum to leave the EU

EUROPEAN UNION MEMBERS BY DATE OF ACCESSION

1958   (EEC)
- Belgium*
- France*
- Germany*
- Italy*
- Luxembourg*
- Netherlands*

1973 (EEC)
- Denmark
- Ireland*
- United Kingdom

1981   (EEC)
- Greece*

1986   (EEC)
- Portugal*
- Spain*

1995 (EU)
- Austria*
- Finland*
- Sweden

2004 (EU)
- Cyprus*
- Czech Republic
- Estonia*
- Hungary
- Latvia*
- Lithuania*
- Malta*
- Poland
- Slovakia*
- Slovenia*

2007 (EU)
- Bulgaria

• Romania
2013 (EU)
• Croatia

*Eurozone members

European Union Candidate countries: Albania, the former Yugoslav Republic of Macedonia, Montenegro, Serbia and Turkey

Potential European Union Candidate countries: Bosnia & Herzegovina, Kosovo

European Free Trade Association (EFTA) Members: Iceland, Liechtenstein, Norway, Switzerland

Customs Unions with EU: Turkey, Andorra, San Marino